DARKNESS to *Light*

WALKING WITH JESUS: A SURVIVOR'S JOURNEY AND A
MOTHER'S LOVE THROUGH TRAUMATIC BRAIN INJURY

SANDRA GIESE FABIAN
MELISA BECHTOLD TENVOORDE

LUCIDBOOKS

To the power of prayer, my loyal and loving family, and the positive attitude and endless determination of my son Tim.

—Sandra

With heartfelt thanks this book is dedicated to my family, friends, and especially my mom for your never-ending support. To Carla who has been my cheerleader all along the way. To Mike for your personal journal entries that gave me so much information and insight. To my co-author Sandy for helping me organize my thoughts and understand my story. And lastly, to my son who has always seen me as just mom.

—Melisa

Table of Contents

Special Thanks

I am truly blessed by the many prayers and by the dedicated people who trusted God to shine through in my miracle of survival. God is faithful.

> *Come to me, all of you who are weary and carry heavy burdens. and I will give you rest.*
>   —Matthew 11:28 (NIV)

We can believe God's trust in our paths as survivors and those who put faith in him to carry us through. Praise God!

                                                    —Melisa

A special thanks to my husband. This project would not have been possible without his patience, support, and willingness to let me try.

                                                    —Sandra

INTRODUCTION:
Melisa

It is a beautiful June morning as I sit on the patio in my comfy papasan chair with my dog by my side. Summer mornings are a special part of the day that I dedicate to God with thanksgiving and prayers for the things that are weighing on my heart.

My name is Melisa, and I am from Minnesota. Starting my summer days outdoors surrounded by the beauty of nature with the rustling of squirrels and the chirping of birds is a gift I give myself as often as possible. As I sit here sipping a vanilla latte from my new pottery mug with a thumb hold—my new favorite mug gifted by a potter friend—I am reflecting on my car accident and traumatic brain injury (TBI) recovery.

The accident was a potentially fatal and horrible event that could have taken my life and shattered the lives of those close to me. However, it became a miraculous chapter in my life. The start of my recovery was sparked by my family's favorite television game show when I finally felt the wheels in my brain begin to reconnect.

Read along with me as I share this story and others from my memoir. I invite you to walk beside me as I tell you about a terrible event that briefly shattered my life and also provide resources and suggestions that have helped my healing. Let's explore this story together as partners, and I encourage you to relate your own journey to mine.

I believe God was at work many times at just the right moments, and I hope this story will help you see God working in your life too. The cliffhanger isn't the beginning of the story but the beginning of the recovery. I will share the peaks and valleys that were life-changing for me in the hope that you will relate them to your own experiences.

My TBI journey and struggles may be similar to yours, but there are likely some differences. Still, through heartbreak and challenges, we can find hope and recognize miracles. We will go through this together, no matter where you are in your recovery. It has been twenty-seven years since my car accident, and I continue to heal from that experience. A TBI diagnosis involves a lifetime of adjustments, but I'm here to tell you they are not all bad. And maybe God is there in the midst of your TBI, waiting for you.

INTRODUCTION:

Sandra

You never forget the experience of getting that call: "There's been an accident . . . we are airlifting . . . come immediately . . . . call other immediate family." It was the call that withheld information like dead or alive, the call that plunged you and your family into terror and chaos.

If you have picked up this book, you may have experienced that same call and found yourself on a difficult journey with an unknown outcome. You might be looking for answers, or you could be feeling terrified, angry, or filled with sorrow. All these emotions are normal and expected, and will likely arrive in varying waves, each one unique to your own circumstances.

I am a mother, and my son was the victim of a traumatic brain injury (TBI). His accident occurred twenty-three years ago when he was twenty-nine years old. His outcome is positive; he has reinvented his future and is now a successful and happy version of himself. This story begins on a curvy, gravel road on a cold, dark, blustery New Year's Eve. It starts with a personal choice and demonstrates the ripple effect of that one decision. It also tells of loyalty, love, and support from family and friends. It shares an inspiring example of courage and the tenacity to survive and thrive.

This is the story of my son's journey with TBI as seen through my eyes and memories. There may be additional stories and perspectives about this journey from family and others close to this experience. But this is my version, and I take responsibility and ownership of the stories and descriptions.

Like most people, my life has been a series of joys and sorrows, successes and failures. From the highest peak to the lowest valley, I have always been blessed by the constant and enduring presence of my Lord and Savior. I have heard His voice speak to me throughout my life, even before I recognized it. Whether I chose to follow His direction or take my own path, His love never failed me. I have often thought about sharing some chapters from my life to connect with the challenges faced by others like you. I believe that as our life events intersect, we weave a pattern that more clearly reveals the hand of God in our everyday lives, decisions, and choices.

I have been a writer in an informal sense for most of my adult life. I have boxes of personal journals that record over fifty years of conversations with God about whatever is on my mind. I have written several personal books for private viewing, and I have been honored to provide ghostwriting services for families to create keepsake books filled with documents, dates, photos, and life stories. However, I have always wanted to write in a more formal way. This is the first book I've written that is out in the world for anyone to read, and frankly, it's a little scary.

This book was born from a chance meeting at my church. I call it a God moment. I had just attended a tai chi class, and as the attendees were leaving the church, I struck up a conversation with a woman young enough to be my daughter. She shared that she had incurred a TBI some decades ago and was frustrated because she didn't know anyone who could relate to her situation. I told her I could relate, and we began to share our perspectives and experiences, which led to a blossoming friendship. From that chance encounter, we both realized that we wanted to share how the Lord had worked in our lives through the TBI and that we both had dreamed of writing a book about it. The idea grew into the book you have in your hand.

My goal for you as you read this book is to find encouragement, insight, humor, and hope. I want you to appreciate the story and how it relates to your own experience. Find the parallels and differences to explore your own questions and concerns. More importantly, I pray that you will hear the voice of God on these pages.

Lastly, I offer this prayer with you:

Father God, bless us this day. Guide our paths, our thoughts, our words, and our deeds. Help us trust Your plan and accept Your will and timing. Assist us each day in letting Your light shine through us, even when we don't feel it. Carry us when we cannot take another step, grant us wisdom when we are confused, and guide us to walk by faith and not by sight in all things. In Jesus's name we pray. Amen.

Melisa's Story
as a TBI Survivor

CHAPTER 1

The Accident

My name is Melisa, and I have a traumatic brain injury. This is my story about survival through the good, the bad, and the ugly; through my challenges, fear, and determination while God was with me the whole way.

I am the youngest of six children. I have five older brothers whose ages ranged from two to sixteen when I was born. My family called me a surprise, spoiled, and tough. My mom used to joke that I was the best mistake she ever made. She told me they had a boy's name picked out, and when she learned she had a baby girl, I was unnamed for two days until my mom remembered my older brother's teacher's name, Melisa, and she thought that sounded perfect.

I was spoiled with love and attention throughout my childhood, which led me to be happy and confident. My oldest brother was my baptismal godfather, and I kept reminding him of this important role as I grew up. When I was two years old, I was a flower girl in his wedding, and then he moved to California. I talked to him on the phone a couple times a month.

My parents were faithful Christians and hard workers throughout their lives. I remember my youngest brother and I kneeling on the linoleum floor in the kitchen, resting our arms on the wooden dining room chairs with our rosaries in hand, and saying the Sorrowful Mysteries, a Lenten rosary. I attended Catholic school from kindergarten through college and developed a strong relationship with God.

When I was six years old and my closest brother was eight, we moved to a hobby farm in the country. We didn't have nearby neighbors we could call to come over and play, so my brother and I played together. As we got older and he had friends over, I was sometimes included in their rough and tough play, which sharpened my skills at sports. All that time playing with my brother is probably why I was one of the first to play kickball at recess, and the boys never said I shouldn't join them.

My parents transformed our hobby farm into a gardener's dream. Mom was busy raising chickens and tending her garden, which was full of colorful fruits, vegetables, and amazing flowers. In the summer, we ate straight from the garden. Our meals included corn on the cob, squash, potatoes, and fresh raspberries or strawberries over vanilla ice cream for dessert. What a treat! I learned from a young age to love the hard work and peaceful joy of gardening. My work ethic and inner strength came from watching my parents be rewarded by the simple pleasures of life.

We were a close family, so when I met my high school and college sweetheart, my parents and brothers were protective of sixteen-year-old me and asked a lot of questions about where we were going and what we planned to do. In the fall of 1994, after eight years of dating through high school and college, we finally got married. My brothers were so excited to call him brother-in-law that after the wedding rehearsal, they all left for the groom's dinner without me. Fortunately, they realized their mistake and came back to pick me up. The next day, after the wedding photos were taken, the men went to the bar across from the church. On their way back, they carried my groom in his white tux above their shoulders, laughing all the way back to the church. It must have been some kind of initiation into the family.

In June 1997, we moved into our new home that we had spent so much time designing and building. My oldest brother had recently moved back from California and was living with us temporarily. In mid-December, I baked chocolate mint crinkles for my first neighborhood Christmas cookie exchange. I hid a couple dozen in our basement so my husband and my brother wouldn't eat them before the holiday celebrations. We had just hosted Christmas and a fun, memorable New Year's Eve party. I was five years into my dream job teaching kindergarten and three years married, eagerly planning my life as a young woman who was fortunate enough to accomplish most of her dreams.

On Sunday, January 4, I enjoyed a pleasant thirty-minute ride to my classroom. Since the kindergartners would be returning to school the next day, I planned to make our classroom inviting and updated. I took pride in decorating it with bright colors and educational bulletin boards. I painted active learning activities on one chalkboard that aligned with our unit of study for the month. January's theme was discovering Antarctica, with a focus on the Emperor and Adélie penguins. I painted icebergs, penguins, and snow.

I always set out the current week's schedule in the heavy-duty mailbox system my dad built for me. It included our daily activities, lessons, and art projects. I did this religiously to ensure everything was ready in case there was a hangup of sorts.

I placed thank you cards for Christmas gifts in my students' mailboxes, set up the January calendar, and updated the weather chart. I changed the very important person (VIP) bulletin board, posted the letter of the week, and put up the Antarctica penguin theme for January. I was teaching in a parochial school where we had welcomed the birth of Christ, so I packed up the nativity scene until I could use it again.

I prepared Buddy Bear, our class stuffed bear, by putting him back in his chair and placing the journal beside him. Buddy Bear always spent Christmas with my family. I finished the journal page of our activities and added our photo taken by the Christmas tree, just like in previous years.

Let me tell you a little about Buddy Bear. He made the front page of the local newspaper a few years back. A kindergartener and their family had taken him on a weekend adventure to Chicago, several states away, and accidentally left Buddy Bear in a restaurant bathroom. The family frantically tracked him down, and the restaurant was happy to eventually send him back to us. On Monday morning in class, Buddy Bear wasn't there. We learned who the new VIP was, discussed our letter of the week, and listened to the news about Buddy Bear's adventure. The kindergartners' prayers and well wishes were heartfelt as we waited two long days for his return. Buddy Bear's wooden chair that my dad had built for him sat next to my rocker. The children noticed and commented throughout our class time that his chair was empty. Looking back now, I wish I had asked them to draw pictures of what they thought Buddy Bear was doing while he was away.

The box with Buddy Bear inside finally arrived, and we placed it in the middle of our circle. The children excitedly counted down from five to one and watched as the box was opened. We found our greatly missed Buddy Bear safely inside. Buddy Bear was pretty spiffy with his gray and blue striped sleeveless sweater. I had asked my mom months before to make a pair of black pants for Buddy with a hole in the back for his golf-ball-sized tail.

Buddy Bear's bag was tucked inside the box as well. His bag included a Buddy Bear news journal, a few easy books for the kindergartners to read to Buddy, and a perfectly sized pillow and blanket. The local newspaper photographed this amazing recovery. The article in our newspaper was pleasant to read, and we were happy to provide such an innocent cover story about his return.

I was amazed and honored when I recently learned that a college professor of mine having seen the article in the local newspaper had used the story of Buddy Bear as an example for how to create a connection between home and school.

On Monday, January 5, 1998, at 5:30 p.m., my life changed suddenly on an icy overpass. I was driving home from a day of teaching when the accident happened. Years before, when I was in high school, my mom was always concerned about driving because we lived in the country. Most of my activities were 10 to 18 miles from home. In the evenings, whether I was at my fun job at the mall selling teenage clothing, at dance practice, or at a sporting event at my high school, I always knew Mom and Dad were waiting for me. Dad was usually asleep in his rocker watching TV, and Mom was knitting or crocheting. I felt secure knowing they were waiting for me. That continued even after I got married.

That Monday, I was running late getting home from school to make dinner. We were excited to celebrate my oldest brother's first day of work since moving back to Minnesota. I took a shortcut that included an overpass. The weather was cold with blowing snow.

That drive home from my school wasn't considered particularly safe on a good day. My mom was always anxious about my drive to and from school and called me before 5:00 each night to be sure I had made it home safely. For years, she warned me never to take an overpass during freezing rain or snow. Moms always know best, and I wish I had listened to her that day. Ironically, my parents were in town shopping that day in the icy weather, and I never received my 5:00 "did you get home safely" call. Instead, my mom's fear became reality that night.

I have no memory of the accident, but I was told that my SUV was hit head on by a car that skidded on an icy patch on the overpass. I was told that one of the first people on the scene was a nineteen-year-old electrician who had recently joined the local Fire and Rescue Squad. When he arrived, he immediately took action and climbed onto my overturned vehicle. He held my head to prevent me from choking on my bloody nose caused by the airbag. I'm thankful for the airbag, my safe vehicle, and most of all his strong, capable, caring hands.

That is where God met me—on an icy overpass on my way home. Years later, the young man became a sheriff. One day, I drove past my neighbor's house and waved like we always did. The sheriff was talking with my neighbor and her little boys in her driveway. She told him who I was, and he immediately wanted to hear more. He asked if I was the person he had helped years ago. He always wondered if I made it. Now he knew.

After hearing about this incredible connection, my neighbor arranged a time for the sheriff and me to finally meet, fourteen years after the accident. When I was thinking about writing my story, I often recalled this important young man who had saved my life. Now I would be able to reach out to him and find out what he remembered about that day. I could ask him a few questions and, most importantly, thank him for his life-saving actions. I was nervous to meet him, like a teenager on my first day of school. At that time, I had been through years of therapy, surgeries, and recovery. He had saved my life, and I wanted him to be proud. Here's what he told me about that day:

> I was working about 2 miles away from the accident scene when the pager went off. I responded immediately to the crash. I believe the roads were quite icy, and the crash happened on the bridge. Your SUV was tipped over on the driver's side, facing eastbound over the eastbound lane of Interstate 94. From what I remember, the top part of your vehicle was over the bridge overpass. A few passersby were there, but I was the first fire and rescue team on the scene. I recall going around the

vehicle near the guardrail of the bridge and finding you unconscious. I'm pretty sure your driver's window was shattered, and you were buckled in. My only job that day was to hold your head, keep your airway clear, and protect your spine from further harm. You had soft spots on your skull, but I don't remember much bleeding. I know it was one of my earlier traumatic crashes. Others arrived and made their way to the back of your vehicle. The crew worked to unbuckle you, lift you out, and carry you to the back of the ambulance. For some reason, I remember you wearing black and white tweed pants because I lifted you out of the driver's seat area.

A TBI, regardless of where or how it happens, is never forgotten by those who witness it. Photos, conversations, and images in your mind bring it all back to life. People close to you will remember who told them about your injury, where they were, and what they were doing when they received the news. You just can't forget some details.

God in the Midst of TBI – When God Is with You

I know my story isn't your story, but if you're like me, you might be learning new things about your TBI story. Many of the things I share in this book are what I learned while writing this book because they were incidents that were never directly shared with me. Many who cared for me during my TBI felt the hurt was too fresh, the pain was too recent, and the memory was too frightening to tell me exactly what happened. Life moved on, and most people assumed I knew the details of my hospital stay when I was in a minimally conscious state. They thought what I didn't know wouldn't hurt me.

You might be in the same boat I was, wondering what else happened, how I reacted to pain, therapies, and daily tasks like eating and using the bathroom. Perhaps your memory starts and ends at different points in time with a gap between what you remember and what others have told you. You might be filled with an unspeakable anxiety, fear, and uncertainty that take hold as your brain continues to heal from the trauma of your accident.

You may be questioning whether you've been told the truth or how much of it you've actually received. You might have been told that you'll improve in the year following your TBI. I still see progress even twenty-seven years after my TBI. I recently had back surgery, and now I have better balance, allowing me to do things more safely.

More important than wondering about the details of your own accident, you might be facing an even bigger question: Where was God? While I cannot speak about the details of your story, I can share mine and tell you exactly where God was the day my vehicle flipped over. He was there with me, keeping breath in my lungs and blood pumping through my veins. He was there in the ambulance as it rushed me to the emergency room, guiding the hands of the paramedics. He was there in the days and months that followed as I relearned all the things my TBI made me forget. He was there then, He's still here now, and I can say with confidence that He was and will be with you.

In Psalm 91:1-2, the psalmist describes God's active protection even when tragedy appears all around: "The one who lives under the protection of the Most High dwells in the shadow of the Almighty. I will say concerning the Lord, who is my refuge and my fortress, my God in whom I trust." My prayer for you is that this psalm isn't just something that sounds nice but is a reality that you've lived. I want you to know the faithfulness of God as you read my story so you might see His faithfulness in your story. He is our refuge and our fortress, the One we can trust to be with us every step of the way.

God isn't finished with you, and He's given you a hope, a future, and a purpose. He is with you still, and you can choose to trust Him yet.

CHAPTER 2

The Hospital

The ambulance rushed me to the hospital where the medical staff took me to the intensive care unit. They put stitches in my head and tried to stabilize me. Ultimately, they decided to put me in a coma where I stayed for nearly two months.

As I began writing this story, I became curious about the details of what happened to me immediately after the accident. I had been curious about that for many years. I contacted the hospital where I was taken and asked for my medical records. Once I received them, I left the records on my table for a couple weeks.

One evening when I was in a calm state of mind, I started to read them. I read that my diagnosis was a severe closed head injury. I learned that I had clenched my jaw tightly, and they couldn't establish an adequate airway. During my ride from the accident scene to the hospital, they used a bag-valve mask and inserted a nasal airway to get oxygen into my lungs. As I read the hospital report, it felt as if I were a witness to my accident.

It is an intriguing phenomenon when you lose a chunk of time from your memory. I had always wondered what happened the night of my accident but had never searched for the details. That information helps me complete some pieces of my puzzle, and twenty-seven years later, I was mentally prepared to read the hospital records. You may feel the urge to uncover your own details; however, it could be shocking or even painful. You will know when the time is right.

While I have no direct memory of the two months after my accident, I was blessed with family, friends, and a husband who journaled through their experiences by my side as the doctors did everything they could to repair and restore the damage to me. I've included excerpts from their journals and their memories in the hope that my story, told through their eyes, will bring to light the reality of my own recovery and also shed light on what your recovery might have been like. While there's much of my story that I'm still coming to terms with, having insights from my husband, Mike, my family, and my friends has given me a better understanding of what my accident was like for them and how they navigated the immediate aftermath.

Mike's Journal – January 5, 1998

At about 4:45, you and I talked on your cell phone about when we were going to have supper together. We agreed that I would meet you at home about 6:00 p.m. I had taken out a pound of ground beef that morning. It was about 5:50 when I called home because I had a strange feeling that you weren't going to be there. I called continually from 5:50

until ten to fifteen minutes after six. At this point, I had a strange feeling that something was wrong. It was only a few minutes later when I received a phone call from the hospital to tell me that my wife had been in a serious accident. At this point, I panicked, swore, yelled, and ran to my car and called the hospital to find out what was actually wrong. They told me you were in critical condition and that your injury was very, very serious. The things that were going through my head were overwhelming.

Mike arrived at the hospital in a few minutes and shortly thereafter was joined by his sister and her children. She would later tell me, "I saw Mike in the emergency room, and when he saw me, he threw his cup of coffee up against the wall and broke down crying. Mike told me the hospital chaplain read you your last rites."

Mike's Journal – January 5, 1998

Monday night, I was allowed in your intensive care unit (ICU) room about 10:00 p.m. I pulled up a chair next to your bed, held your hand, and did not move until 6:00 a.m. I did not close my eyes or let go of your hand, and prayed nonstop. The next day, Tuesday, you were put deeper into your coma because your brain was overstimulated and beginning to swell. I was not able to stay with you that night.

My mom shared with me later that during this very early time after my accident, she had prayed the Saint Therese prayer:

> O little Therese of the Child Jesus, please pick for me a rose from the heavenly gardens and send it to me as a message of love. Oh, Little Flower of Jesus, ask God to grant the favors I now place with confidence in your hands. St. Therese, help me to always believe as you did in God's great love for me, so that I might imitate your "Little Way" each day. Amen.

In the Catholic tradition, this prayer holds value as a powerful devotional prayer rooted in the saint's promise to send roses as a sign of her heavenly intercession. Seeing a rose gave reassurance that your prayer would be answered. After my mom prayed that prayer, she began finding roses everywhere. She told my family that I would be alright, that God loved me, and that He would heal me. Mike and my brothers were shocked with mom's confidence but hoped what she said would be true.

I was told that as the days passed, even though I was in a coma, I was becoming overstimulated from all the flowers, gifts, and bustle of visitors all wishing me well. As a result, the flowers and other gifts were removed, visitors were limited to two at a time, and they placed cooling ice blankets under and over my body to help me regulate my body temperature. Although I wasn't consciously aware of the gifts and visits at the time, I am now overwhelmed by the outpouring of love and support I received.

Prayer was always a constant resource for my family. It was a way for them to organize their thoughts, wishes, and dreams for my recovery. Reflecting on these comments the first few days after my accident, I realize that those who loved me had to watch me struggle and face the uncertainty that I might not survive. I feel sad hearing about these memories, yet I know that God was with them.

On my first day of high school, I had met a girl named Sarah. At the end of that day, we had some free time, so we sat outside on the granite steps and started what would become a lifelong friendship. After my accident, Sarah was a regular visitor at the hospital. She wrote an entry in the visitors' journal.

Sarah's Journal Entry – January 10, 1998

You are such a wonderful friend. I love you with all my heart. My mom said out of all my friends, you were the one with the most spunk and energy. Please remember that I will be here even when you don't want me around. I can't wait to hear you laugh. You are looking better. You began moving your arms and feet today, and you are moving your tongue around.

Mike's Journal – January 12, 1998

It is now Monday morning, and you are going to have some tests done. I told the nurses you were claustrophobic because you are going to get an MRI. I asked if you could be put into an open-sided one, but they don't have one. I was telling you not to worry and that I would be thinking about you. When you got back from your test, the nurses told me that the doctors had said that they knew you were claustrophobic by the way you reacted to the test. It is now 3:30 on Monday afternoon, and the snow has stopped falling. It's been very cold temperatures, 40–60 below zero. I'm playing Vince Gill CDs. The doctors said it would be a good idea to play music that you liked . . . to get you out of the coma.

This entry surprised me because I remember a shared experience Mike and I had years ago. We visited a farm that offered fun activities centered on the farm and the barnyard. It was a sunny fall day as we walked through the crackling dried leaves toward the laughter of children and the smell of hot apple cider brewing. We were young and adventurous, and decided to crawl through the dark, enclosed tunnel inside the hog barn. In the middle of the experience, I realized that with all the people in the tunnel, I couldn't go forward or backward, and I had a panic attack. Since then, I have had a fear of tight places.

It's interesting for me to realize that even while in a coma, I must have had a sense of my enclosed surroundings. I don't associate that experience with trying to wake up from my coma, but I do connect it to some form of subconscious awareness. You might wonder if we can sense our family's and friends' presence, and I believe we do. From my experience, there is a reaction or memory of past experiences, and there is comfort in familiar touches, voices, and sounds. I encourage you to stay physically present with your loved one as much as possible.

Mike's Journal – January 15, 1998, 3:45 p.m.

I am so excited and happy. You are doing so well. You are so strong. Your eyes are wide open, but you do not focus. You looked around the room and squeezed my hand. Last night, they took a drain tube out of your head. This was the first true sign that you were going to be OK. For the last few days, they have been putting you in a chair that sits you upright; this chair allows all the fluid in your lungs to drain. They have also started putting you in high-top shoes to keep your feet from cramping. I was told there was a worry about damage to your brain, that you might have mood swings and other personality things.

Reflecting on my prediction about mood swings and personality changes after my TBI, this is what I experienced. Before my TBI, I was organized, kind, and a fun-loving presence in most situations. I had many friends and enjoyed outdoor activities like tennis, swimming, biking, and long walks. When I regained awareness after my TBI, I was unsure of my thoughts and feelings and didn't have a plan for what was coming next. I felt uncertain about my emotions and struggled with reactions from my loved ones. I was short-tempered and angry about my circumstances, and I couldn't return to the real me fast enough. I was disappointed in myself and my immediate reactions to daily circumstances and interactions. I felt isolated, sad, and frustrated.

I have a friend named Karen. We met in our freshman year of high school. We had classes together, including extracurricular dance class, and I often stayed at her house after school activities because she lived closer to the school than my family did. After both of us got married, the four of us continued to do things together as couples. She recorded this in her journal.

Karen's Journal – January 20, 1998

I am not quite sure if I truly will have you read this, but it is therapeutic for me to write to you just as it is to see you. I am very sad tonight, feeling very lonesome for you. I cannot imagine how Mike feels. Today I am feeling so hopeless. I cannot imagine why you're not out of your coma. I'm wondering, are you okay? Do you know what is happening? If you do, I hope that you know how much you are loved. We are all waiting on your every move. I love you and miss you. Please come back. Regarding the February 14th weekend, the four of us were planning an outing—we still are going to spend it together, whether you're in the hospital or at home. This accident has really made me think about life, death, immortality, and mortality. It is so unpredictable. Something I also wonder about is whether or not you have spoken with God. They do say that some people in a coma come awake and speak of the light and speak with

God. Who knows? I do know that if God had you reflect on your life, you would do it. And you should be proud. You are such a wonderful person, a big heart, very smart, generous, supportive, caring, loving, trusting, great listener, and most of all funny. If you have taught me anything, it is to laugh often and to be optimistic. I love you. Karen.

Mike's Journal – January 21, 1998

Prayers came from everyone and everywhere. Four different places: churches, four different schools, the Poor Clare Monastery, radio stations, and the 700 Club TV station. You have so much support, love, and prayer that God has been with you this whole time.

As I reflect on the depth of prayers and well wishes I received at that time from family, friends, and even people I didn't know, I realize I was extremely blessed by God and am so thankful. Before my TBI, I may not have noticed all the blessings in my life, but looking back now, they were plentiful. Each situation is uniquely yours, but kindness and support can be found in many ways—whether from medical staff, the chaplain, or even the person who delivers your meals—to brighten your day. When you feel lonely or alone, I encourage you to take a moment to reflect on the hidden kindnesses in your day. I believe it will bring you joy.

We can always depend on God for strength and support. Isaiah 40:29 (NIV) says, "He gives strength to the weary and increases the power of the weak."

Mike's Journal – January 26 and 27, 1998

You have been staying stable. The CT scans and X-rays you've been getting daily show that your condition was not getting worse but actually getting better. This is what the doctors said was good news. With your injury, the first seventy-two hours were the crucial hours. They said that your condition would be getting worse and worse before it got better. The news that you are stable was really good news. I was told that with this injury, there was going to be some damage to your brain, with memory, thought process, and mood swings. They told me this, but also said they weren't sure how long it would last. They said you are going to need therapy and a lot of work.

The doctors knew I would need a lot of therapy, but with TBI, knowing exactly how much work would be required is more or less a guessing game. The hospital notes say that on Tuesday, February 3, 1998, I was taken by ambulance to an inpatient rehabilitation facility about two hours away to continue my care and recovery. My family told me they followed the ambulance. Even though I moved facilities, the visits from Mike, my parents, and other family and friends continued. There was more work to do, but for my husband, family, and friends, it seemed like recovery was becoming something they could genuinely hope for.

God in the Midst of TBI – The Power of Prayer

Songs like "Somebody Prayed" by Crowder resonated with me. The words reassured me of the power of prayer in a hospital during the first weeks after my accident, and I am so thankful. However, it has taken me years to recognize these miracles.

The truth is, there are no small parts of the story God is writing through you, and there are no small prayers. From the smallest prayer whispered by acquaintances to the short, repetitive prayers prayed a thousand times by close friends and family as they watch over you in the ICU, they bear witness to a miracle yet to happen. My hope is that you'll take the time to notice the small glimpses of miracles in your own progress by taking notice of the thousand prayers that covered you even when you were unaware.

Without even knowing the prayers that are said on our behalf, we are lifted up. God is with us every step of the way and in each part of our journey. My prayer for you is that you hold onto the truth that God hears the prayers of those who have prayed and are praying for you. He asks us to pray because He wants us to come to Him with our needs, and He wants us to bring our loved ones to Him so He might heal them. Like the friends who lowered their paralyzed friend down through the roof so Jesus could heal him, our friends bring us to Jesus in prayer that He might heal us.

Psalm 77:14 (NIV) says, "You are the God who performs miracles." We survivors are the direct recipients of a miracle. Even during our coma, God was with us, and I am in awe as I picture God holding His hands above me, working a miracle.

God's intervention guided me on a path to recovery that was only possible because of His healing work in me. It is humbling to imagine the heartache my family endured, and I am so thankful for the promise they clung to and grateful that they never stopped praying.

There were times in my story, especially early on, when the doctors and even my family thought my story had come to an end. My guess is that you've experienced similar moments in your own story and may be going through one now. I don't say this to minimize your story, but I say it to remind you of a truth that is true even in the darker parts of our journey with TBI: God is present, and whatever happens next is God's will for you.

The chances are high that your life after your TBI will not be the same as it was before. I know mine hasn't been. There may be things you used to do that you can no longer do or parts of your personality you can't access anymore. Whether internally or externally, TBI leaves a lasting impact. However, God has not wasted any part of my story, and He won't waste any part of yours. Although God's path is different for each of us, when we seek His will during recovery, we find purpose beyond the pain and healing greater than our wounds.

CHAPTER 3

Inpatient Therapy

On February 3, 1998, when I was transported by ambulance to an inpatient rehabilitation hospital, my condition was stable, although I was not yet responsive. My family and friends continued to visit me regularly.

I was still unresponsive even though my eyes were open, and the rehabilitation staff began various therapies in hopes of stimulating my brain. However, I remained in an unresponsive state. I am humbled to read journal entries from so many people who continued to visit and pray for me. I believe that even though our conscious memory isn't active, our subconscious still knows and senses that we are loved.

Mike recorded this while I'd just begun my time at the inpatient rehabilitation clinic.

Mike's Journal - February 13, 1998

It's been a while since I've written to you now. I guess it's because every time I do, I feel terrible and get depressed. Things have been really hard for me; it's hard to explain just what I'm feeling and going through. It's Friday morning, and I'm in your hospital room. I took the whole day off so I could spend it with you. Tomorrow is Valentine's Day. I could not imagine spending Valentine's Day without you.

My mom later told me that after about three weeks, I still wasn't showing signs of response or improvement. The hospital personnel advised my family to start looking for a long-term care facility for me. This event saddened all as Mike began searching for an appropriate place with nursing care.

Happily, my new life began on Sunday, February 22, 1998. My youngest brother and his wife stopped at a drugstore to pick up something to pass the time while visiting me. I believe God worked through my brother. They bought a handheld electronic version of the *Wheel of Fortune* game, the game show my parents and I watched frequently on TV. Being a contestant had always been and still is on my bucket list. They said I was propped up in a wheelchair, and they sat on either side of me playing the game and spelling words.

As my brother was spelling a word, I reached over and touched the screen to correct his spelling. At that moment, my brother got very excited and told the nurses, "She's in there." I'm thankful they left the game for me to continue playing and to wake up my brain. I had watched *Wheel of Fortune* regularly, and the connection stimulated my brain, helping the wheels start turning in the right direction.

My first clear memory is of a day when my mom took me to therapy. I wasn't speaking and was in a wheelchair, but when we returned to my room, I stood up in the restroom in front of the mirror as I had probably done many times before. This time I looked in the mirror and noticed that my head was shaved. I turned to my mom and gestured, wondering where my hair was. She explained that I had been in a car accident and that my head had been shaved for a procedure done earlier in my recovery.

As my mom wheeled me out of the restroom, I remember noticing that the walls of my room were decorated with artwork, and I knew it was from the students in my classroom. The artwork sparked my memory and brought back warm memories of my students, my classroom, and my projects. Thinking about all of that, especially working with my students, was comforting to me.

I remember riding in my wheelchair down the hospital hallway with dull white tile floors and plaster walls painted a tan color that felt sterile and cold. However, when the elevator doors opened to the therapy waiting room, I was comforted by soft yellow walls and shades of warm blue in the rugs and pillows. The atmosphere gave me a sense of connection and familiarity.

Various members of my family often accompanied me to therapy, and I remember feeling comforted by the young lady at the reception desk because she looked like my niece. I recall trying to tell my family to notice that similarity, but at that moment, I couldn't get them to understand. It was exasperating each time we entered that space and checked in with the sweet young lady at the reception desk, but it wasn't until I could speak that I could explain why I always seemed frustrated when we encountered my niece's twin. It all made sense to them now as the wonder of what I was trying to communicate came to a close.

Once I successfully played electronic *Wheel of Fortune* and my family knew I was aware and wanted to communicate, my dad asked the nurses for a letter board so we could try to interact by spelling words together. Using the letter board made me feel very relieved, but it was tiring. I also remember feeling both relief and frustration because there was an urgency to communicate, but my family struggled to understand what I was trying to say. Looking back, I feel sorry that my mom was working so hard to write down the letters as fast as I was pointing to them. When she missed an important piece, I pointed to the "end of the word box" to separate the letters so I could form words instead of a long string of letters. I would sigh and start over, and she would struggle to keep up so we could finally communicate.

During this awakening period, I also remember sitting and listening to many conversations. It felt like I was in an audience. I don't remember specific conversations or topics, just the general buzz of people I loved who were talking to each other. I remembered that I used to be an active participant in conversations, and I felt frustrated because at that time I was an onlooker. But I was thrilled to watch and listen to the entertainment their conversations provided me. I realized that it's better to be an active listener, and I was doing just that.

TBI recovery can be frustrating, especially when we can't express ourselves outwardly while we're thinking. I felt like I was in a bubble. I was enclosed. I could breathe, but I couldn't express myself. I couldn't get my family to understand what I was thinking or hear my thoughts.

My high school friend, Sarah, visited me often after work. One afternoon, she came in, hung up her coat, and said, like she did on each visit, "Hi Missy," and to her surprise, I responded in a whispery voice, "Hi." She was so excited that she called my home phone number from memory, put the phone to my mouth, and told me to talk. I spoke again in a kind of whisper, saying, "Hi Mom." I could hear my mom's breath hitch as she was overwhelmed with happiness.

On March 3, my mom wrote in Mike's journal, "The Lord has answered our prayers and petitions. I have my daughter back."

As I became more aware and alert, I remember my doctors telling me I had five things to do before I could go home. I needed to walk, talk, feed myself, dress myself, and use the bathroom. I was determined and anxious to go home, so I tackled the therapy with all my might. Within two weeks, I had accomplished all five things.

During therapy sessions, I struggled because I knew what I was supposed to do and wanted to do it quickly. The speech and walking were the most challenging of the five skills. I realize I needed to master all five to function in my normal daily life. Balance remains a scary issue that still rears its ugly head from time to time, but fortunately, my speech skills came back at a pleasing rate.

A note I want to share about speaking is the vast difference in how I sounded when I began to talk. My old voice never returned. It's hard to know how we actually sound since voicemails and recordings sound different from how we hear ourselves speak. Until I heard family and friends comment on the change, I was unaware of it. It was simply one more thing I had to accept to embrace the new me.

As I was working on this chapter, I believe the Lord led me to this beautiful statement by an unknown author that can relate to my and perhaps your recovery as well. "I'm thankful He is the author of my story. He lovingly writes in the hard parts that show me His care and provision, so that I learn to trust Him more."

The room designated for speech therapy felt like a long, narrow, windowless room, and it made me feel uneasy. I felt anxious because I didn't know how to teach myself to talk. I was learning to form the sounds for words as I was waking up my vocal cords. This was the most difficult part for me because I love to talk, and for some reason, I wasn't able to say anything. It felt like I couldn't figure out which part of talking I was doing wrong. I remember when I had to swallow a camera so the doctors could check my vocal cords. They were still swollen, but there was no cause for alarm, so I was reassured I would be able to talk again soon.

The therapy continued, and I worked hard to use my hands effectively. I was trying to figure out how to use my right hand, but it would not do what I wanted it to do. I had always been right-handed, and it did not occur to me to try using my left hand at that time. However, later, as my mom watched my frustration, she suggested I try to use my left hand. To my surprise, it worked pretty well, and I became a lefty. I guess that was just another change I was going to make that would help me return to the "me" I wanted to be so badly.

During recovery, we have many tasks to accomplish in order to return to our life. Sometimes changing the variable or the process can lead to success. Were you able to accomplish a task that you could no longer do by switching the variable or altering how it is done to find success in a different way? When we are born, our brains develop extra cells that remain on standby; they become active during times like brain injury when they are able to adapt and take over for the brain cells that have been damaged.

There were activities to help strengthen my small motor skills. The most memorable task was tying my shoes. I was a kindergarten teacher and had taught many five- and six-year-olds to do the same. In fact, my dad had made thin wooden manipulative shoes with actual laces for students to take home and practice. I thought about my teaching experiences and used the same techniques in my therapy session. Proudly, I tied my shoe on the very first try.

I wanted people to see me as the same person I was before the accident. I hoped I could become that person again. I now realize that I was aware of my car accident and my urgency to succeed during therapy, and it felt like a rush of rain washing over me. You may experience similar feelings, and it's helpful to recognize them. Looking back at my accident, I realize that before January 5, 1998, I rarely felt emotions like fear, urgency, struggle, or the embarrassment of certain behaviors, and now I still have those feelings. At this point, I am grateful to be able to feel those things because I believe it is better to have those emotions and overcome them than never to have had them at all.

I encourage you to notice all your feelings, whether right or wrong, good or bad as you recover. There will be smiles and moments like "I got it" and times when you think, "This is too hard," or you even want to give up. You should recognize growth and feel pride in every small step of progress. Some tasks will require your full mental and physical effort and will go better on some days than others. Tackle those difficult challenges on days when you feel capable.

I remember having therapy three times a day. It was my work. I also remember that when I was teaching, I never looked forward to the end of the day because I loved teaching so much. In therapy, I kept checking the clock, which seemed to be strategically placed out of my line of sight. Even so, I watched the clock during all my sessions and counted down the time for each one. Every activity felt like it was draining my brain. However, there were some moments along my recovery journey that kept me going, giving me something to look forward to. One such moment was when my two brothers—numbers two and three in the family lineup (my mom used to lovingly refer to my brothers by their birth order since there were five of them, especially as she got older ☺)—who came to visit me during my recovery at St. Kinney, which was an 80-minute drive from them. They stopped for gas on their way to visit me, and while there, they bought $5 worth of pull tabs and made a promise to each other that if they won, they'd give the winnings to me. To their surprise, they did win a good amount and were overjoyed to bless me with it. I later used those winnings toward my window treatments fund when I returned home and finally felt up to finishing my home décor.

Their thoughtfulness and generosity during that time still means so much to me.

Finally, on Friday, March 14, I was delighted to find out that I would be released for a trial visit at home for the weekend. Mike wheeled me to the door where the car was parked. I felt like I was escaping from the hospital's strict routine for the last two and a half months. We had over an hour drive to get home, and as we entered the freeway, my ears were popping like they do on an airplane. The car seemed to be moving so fast because I hadn't moved faster than a walking pace for so long. I felt excited to get back to the new home we had just finished building shortly before my accident. Mike had music playing on the radio, and as we traveled from town to town, the simple task of changing the radio station gave me a new sense of independence.

As we pulled into our driveway, I saw a big welcome home sign on the front porch. It looked like a party. We parked in the garage, and I was greeted by our dog, a golden retriever, who was so happy to see me, just as I was to see her. Mike had brought her to visit me once while I was in rehab, and I was overjoyed. They had told him a visit from a pet would be beneficial.

I tentatively walked up the steps to enter our home. When I opened the door, I saw that our Christmas tree was still standing exactly as I had decorated it back in December. It made me laugh because it was March, and there was still a Christmas tree. As I moved through the house, I went straight to the kitchen, my favorite place. Later, Mike and I were joined by our family. They were all so excited to see me. One memory that is especially sweet to me is the warm hug I received from my stoic father-in-law that day. This feeling of finally being at home was joyful. What a wonderful way to start the weekend.

We went to church that Sunday with Mike pushing me in a wheelchair. We sat in our usual pew, although I was at the end in the wheelchair. In our tradition, we receive communion every Sunday. I felt embarrassed yet grateful when the priest brought communion to me in my wheelchair.

Sunday evening, as we drove back to the rehab facility, I wondered if I would be able to be discharged the next day. On Monday morning, I received the best news ever when the doctor came into my room and told us I was ready to be discharged. We packed all the cards, gifts, and artwork, and headed home to continue our lives. We all have memories of the day we return home. Those moments will hopefully stay with us for a long time. It can be easy to recall monumental happenings years later.

God in the Midst of TBI – When God Begins to Heal You

In her daily devotional, *Jesus Calling*, Sarah Young shares a verse and comment from Philippians 4:13 that resonates with me. "I have strength for all things in Christ who empowers me [I am ready for anything and equal to anything through Him who infuses inner strength into me. I am self-sufficient in Christ's sufficiency]." At that moment when I was going home, I was scared. I was afraid I would disappoint my friends and family. I worried they wouldn't love me as much as before if I couldn't become the person I was. I won't downplay the internal battle you will face as you recover. But I believe we all have inner strength we can draw from. I encourage you to dig deep and find your inner strength because it's there.

Psalm 23 is well known for its comforting words of encouragement. As I read it, the truth comes full circle. The Lord is my Shepherd; the Lord shepherded me even when I didn't realize He was there. I have what I need. He gave me what I needed and allowed my body to rest and my brain to heal. Even when I go through the darkest valley, even in the early days after my accident when there was worry I might not survive, He was there. Only goodness and faithful love will pursue me all the days of my life; He protected, restored, and even directed me to come back to this world.

Please take time to notice the message in Psalm 23:6 (CEV): "Only goodness and faithful love will pursue me all the days of my life, and I will dwell in the house of the Lord as long as I live." This verse reminds us of God's steadfast love for us. If we've put our trust in Him, we are His kids and get all the privileges of life in His house. In God's house, living as His kids, we are forever secure, even if we face hard things in this life. We can know that His goodness and love will pursue us beyond anything this world can throw at us. In God's house and in God's love, we live securely.

In the moments when it feels like you'll be overwhelmed by the weight of your TBI, depend on the strength that God provides. His love is more than enough to handle our hurts, worries, anxieties, and concerns. As God begins to heal us, we'll find that there are still so many things left about our recovery that we wish He'd go ahead and hurry up with. Yet as He heals us, we can rest secure that He will heal us in His time and in His way, both inwardly and outwardly.

A colleague at work had a family member with a TBI. I supported the family by buying a T-shirt that I relate to, and maybe you will too: "You have no idea what strength it takes to wake up each and every day to battle my own body and mind." Trust that you aren't alone in the fight, and trust that God is at work in your recovery and will complete the work He began.

CHAPTER 4
Outpatient Therapy

We left the rehab facility around 10:00 a.m. on March 17, St. Patrick's Day. On the drive home, my first request to Mike was this: "Let's stop and eat and make it feel like a date." My favorite meal of the day has always been breakfast. That day, I ordered a ham and cheese omelet with pancakes and a side of fruit. The experience was stupendous. Not only was it St. Patrick's Day, but it was our first date at the start of our new life. By the way, my pancakes were not green.

After breakfast, we drove the remaining miles home and talked about how life would unfold with work schedules and my ongoing therapy. As we neared home, we shifted the conversation to our dog, Matie. We had previously discussed breeding her at a game farm that Mike frequented. We agreed that the plan was still in progress, and I was so excited about this process.

I had never been involved in breeding before, but when I was a child, our German shepherd was pregnant when we adopted her. Raising those puppies was a wonderful experience on the farm but not as easy in town where I lived now. That summer, we had Matie bred and kept one of the puppies. We named her Bailey. She would be part of our family for twelve years.

Once the puppies were born, I found the experience to be therapeutic. I loved feeding them, cleaning them, playing with them, and trying my hand at puppy potty training. We even took the litter of puppies camping once. The puppies needed me, and they didn't care about my TBI disabilities. It was rewarding because I could focus on something besides my own recovery.

Coming back home after camping, I knew tasks were waiting for me. Since we had just moved into our new house before my accident, I still needed to figure out where things should be stored. I realized it was time to put the Christmas tree and decorations away because it was now March. Finding storage, unpacking, and getting familiar with my home was my first priority.

We had hosted a New Year's Eve party a few days before my accident. I had tucked away cookies downstairs for a cookie exchange before Christmas. Now I found them, and they were no longer edible. Mike's reaction to the saved cookies was obvious: "If I had known they were hidden there, they would have already been eaten."

Walking into my house felt a little like the first day I had walked through the doors. The house was clean and crisp but still a blank canvas because I hadn't had the time to add my personal touch with window treatments and wall colors. I was also overwhelmed because it seemed larger than I remembered, and our bedroom was on the second floor, making the stairs a challenge and even frightening for me.

Maybe you have faced some of these same challenges with steps, balance, and the need for handrails and other safety measures. I still prefer a handrail when taking steps, and I don't anticipate that changing. Accepting these circumstances is part of the healing process. That may take years or even a decade, like mine, but you will identify with the new beautiful you.

Over time, you will develop the ability to anticipate things that might cause difficulties, and sometimes you may choose to reroute your path entirely. For example, I remember a time when we were in a mall. I was trying to step onto a single-file escalator going down, but I couldn't take that first step. I tried several times with Mike coaching me, and as the people lined up behind us, Mike finally said, "Let's go find the elevator."

The first day at home, I accomplished some tasks and felt productive. As the first week went on, I felt an urgency to establish a normal routine. I had mixed emotions about how things would turn out. Once the excitement of returning home faded, I started to feel angry about my circumstances. My normal routine had always been to get up early, make coffee, feed the dog, turn on the morning news, plan dinner, and head off to work. But now, with my fear of driving, no car available, no teaching, and ongoing physical and mental recovery, I was relying on others to help me navigate my life.

Mike had arranged for me to start therapy at home because I wasn't yet able to drive. I had two therapies: occupational therapy (OT) for fine motor skills and physical therapy (PT) for walking and balance. When the therapists left, they gave me exercises to practice. I remember two main things. For OT, I had to place clothespins around an ice cream pail they gave me to practice on. For PT, I worked on walking independently on different surfaces and stairs, and trying to develop a smooth gait. It was not easy to complete the therapy tasks as often as they recommended. I lacked motivation, and sometimes success didn't come.

I know it's hard to do one more thing when you're just trying to live life as you used to. Concentration can be mentally exhausting. It was tough for me at times and maybe for you as well. Sometimes you just need a nap. Naps definitely helped me. During our recovery, I believe that quiet and rest support healing. The brain needs time to recharge and recover quite a bit over the next few months. Give yourself a break; things are going to take longer, and that's okay.

I had to remind myself of Isaiah 40:29 (NIV): "He gives strength to the weary and increases the power of the weak." During my recovery, I have often felt tired and weak. This verse reminds me that even when I feel weak and helpless, I can trust that God will provide the strength I need. Through trial and error, I realize that if I slow down and listen to God, He is helping me notice that the slower I go, the more successful and accurate I am. I will always be the slowest walker and the slowest at eating. I try to keep up, do my best, and not get discouraged with myself. It is comforting to have people around who understand and accept you completely because they help you feel solid and confident.

I was lucky to have friends and family to support me. They drove me to appointments, helped me with shopping, and even took me out for a few lunch dates. When I got home from the hospital, I needed new clothes that fit since I had lost a lot of weight. My friends picked me up, and we had a girls' day of shopping and catching up, just like old times. They helped me pick out clothes, and we all giggled, wondering if they'd fit. The kindness of my friends warmed my heart. It made me feel normal again, like I was getting back to being myself.

As Mike and I began getting back into our normal social life, we gathered with some of our closest friends at a cabin for a couple's retreat. It was still early in my recovery, and my hair was slowly growing back. I was unsteady on my feet and nervous about stairs, but these friends accepted me as I was. As I packed for the trip, I felt a mix of nervousness and excitement about being away from home, but I was comforted because Mike was with me. Although I was beginning to feel like my old self, looking at the photos from that time reminds me that I was just starting to become the new me.

As you try to reenter a normal life, you will encounter a variety of people. Some can take anything on and see beyond your new handicaps or unusual behaviors. Others may be more sensitive to those changes, and it might take them a while to adjust, even as they truly want to be supportive. Be open to any kindness offered, and over time, you will create your own new normal. Some of these TBI characteristics will stay, while others will be refined and softened into your new mannerisms.

There are some characteristics that can occur after a TBI, such as uncontrollable urges—being impulsive, experiencing aggression, or being angry. A positive aspect of my recovery was my urge to laugh, maybe because I was always a happy person before my TBI, but I'm not entirely sure. My family knew about this urge and would try to trigger my burst of laughter. There are three instances that come to mind. The first was at a dinner at my house. As I took a sip of red wine, my family intentionally said something funny to make me laugh.

To my dismay, I spit red wine all over the table and immediately blamed them for making me laugh. The second time this happened, we were driving to a Fourth of July parade. I was in the passenger seat with a cup of vanilla cappuccino when someone said something funny. I laughed and sprayed the beverage all over the dashboard while my family laughed. Another time, without any encouragement, I thought of something funny at church and couldn't control myself as I began to laugh. My family just looked at me with crooked smiles and shook their heads.

Throughout your recovery, you may experience impulses and reactions to situations that you didn't have before your injury. They are normal. Over time, you will find that you can control those impulses and learn how to navigate and avoid certain thoughts that need to be contained in specific situations.

A few weeks after I came home, I was taking something out of my freezer for dinner that evening. It felt like progress because I was getting back into the habit of planning dinner. My mom instilled this habit in me because she always planned dinner for her large family. I always knew dinner was on her mind early in the day when something was thawing on the counter. For the first four weeks after I was home, my mom helped me make dinner, and then I was able to do everything on my own.

The first meal I made solo was my mom's lasagna recipe, which was also Mike's favorite. This marked the start of my new routine of cooking dinner like I used to, and what a rewarding way to end the day. I was back in my home with a routine taking shape, and I was relearning new ways to move around my house and handle daily skills safely. I slept well in my own bed, knowing that the hospital chapter was now behind me.

Mike felt relief getting back to work, but I was feeling a little trapped because I wasn't able to drive and needed help with everyday tasks. My mom visited a few days a week to keep me company, clean, help prepare meals, and ensure I was eating properly. Swallowing was still sensitive, so I ate soft foods. A few favorites were puffed corn because it dissolved in my mouth. Pudding and Jell-O were also my go-to foods. I was discovering new favorite beverages, foods, and TV shows that helped pass the time and bring me a sense of contentment. Looking back at my recovery, I can see the silver lining and realize I was capable of doing much more than I gave myself credit for at the time.

If you are struggling to feel positive about your progress as you recover, think back to where you started—day one, week one, week two, and so on. Looking back, you'll see that you're making progress even if it seems like small steps.

I finished home therapy in about three weeks and transitioned to outpatient therapy at a local facility. I continued to work on my fine motor skills such as my penmanship, eating, and personal care. I did this for roughly six weeks until I completed the therapy. At that point, I was advised that my current job was to rest and allow my brain to keep healing.

I started visiting my classroom as my therapy advanced and I began showing signs of independence. My mom drove me to and from the school. From mid-April until the end of May, I spent a few hours twice a week observing my substitute teacher run the classroom. That experience was both rewarding and painful—being there but unable to perform as I once did. It took time for me to get used to myself, and I think back to how kindergarteners are judgment-free. Even though my hair was very short, my voice was soft and raspy, and my movements were different, I loved their innocent acceptance as they hugged me and welcomed me back.

At the end of each school year, we always had kindergarten graduation. I loved planning that celebration. After graduation that spring, my students' parents gave me heartfelt recognition for being able to attend the kindergarten graduation ceremony. That memory touches my heart every time I think of it.

Before the year was over, the principal asked to observe my teaching. We chose the first-grade classroom. I was using my left hand at the chalkboard, and after the observation, the principal remarked that I was using my left hand to write. She asked about my left hand dominance, and I chuckled, saying that my brain had decided after my accident that I was going to be a lefty. Even though I would have loved to return to my classroom, I decided to take the following year off to continue healing and undergo a foot surgery my doctor had recommended.

As the school year ended, I returned to my summer pastimes as I had always done. Gardening has always been a hobby for me in the spring and summer seasons. I spent June beautifying the landscape of our new yard. Gardening makes me feel an overwhelming sense of peace and energy. I enjoyed planting new flowers that brought life and color to the yard.

What relaxes you? Where is your happy place? There is value in seeking out the simple things and quiet places in your life.

Those places offer you solace where you can recharge and focus on new beginnings. Remember that heavy hearts are real. Things that weigh you down feel heavier than pounds. Our bodies are conditioned to have muscles that perform under challenging conditions, but in order to bear up under the weight, you need moments that bring rest.

As we recover, our hearts and self-confidence are not always prepared for the hurtful thoughts we have about ourselves. I find it easy to insult myself, and maybe you do too. But a friend recently told me, "When you insult yourself, you are insulting my friend." This comment made me think and inspired me to improve my attitude of self-deprecation and be gentle with myself. Recovering from a TBI is hard work, and we need to give ourselves grace.

Toward the end of the summer, I finally gained the courage to start driving again. I was scared to get back behind the wheel because of my accident and spent more time in the slow lane than I normally would have. At this point, my new left-handed dominance and right-sided weakness really became evident. In addition to managing seat belts and mirror adjustments, it was awkward using my left hand, especially when I tried to take a drink from a beverage in the center console.

I was planning to return to teaching, but I first needed to have that foot surgery. My TBI had affected the function of my right foot. I had hammer toes and bunions, which made walking excruciating. In October 1998, I had the first of many surgeries on my foot. After that surgery and the follow-up physical therapy, I was able to walk with less pain, which was a relief.

Right now, I am very grateful that I can speak again, walk, and use my hands for writing, cooking, and working in my flower garden. However, I still long for better balance and smoother strides when I walk. I hear others comment about my old witty personality and cognitive sharpness. I want to be able to run, skip, swim, and dance like before. My fear of another head injury has kept me off my bike, but a new friend introduced to the security and comfort of riding a recumbent bike. A silver lining it is! I remember the person with great balance who now can smile. I struggle with the physical and mental confidence to attempt many activities, but I am aware of the strength and motivation I still have among the new challenges and activities I encounter.

I don't know where you are in your recovery. You might still be in therapy, at home trying to figure out your next step, or years down the road and able to look back. Wherever you are in your recovery, I encourage you to take inventory of where you began. Give yourself credit for what you can do instead of focusing on what you are not able to do yet. The confident desire that is in your spirit will drive you to succeed and conquer many challenges.

You're still here and able to read this, and that is hope enough. The bottom line is that this journey never truly ends. You'll keep making progress, and over time you'll be amazed at the improvements you see. My advice is to stay strong and keep working on the new you. Focus on the things you can do, the progress you are making, and then leave the rest for God to sort out.

God in the Midst of TBI – When God Restores You

I am reminded of the story of the miracle of the blind man found in Luke 18:38–42 (CEV). The story tells of a beggar sitting on the roadside near Nazareth where Jesus was walking. He cried out to Jesus, saying, "Jesus, Son of David, have mercy on me!" (v. 38). The crowd told the blind man to be quiet, but he kept calling out for Jesus.

Jesus stopped and asked, "What do you want me to do for you?" (v. 40). The blind man replied, "Lord, I want to see" (v. 41). Jesus said, "Receive your sight; your faith has saved you" (v. 42).

In this story about healing, Jesus instantly heals the blind man. We TBI survivors have a different journey. Instead of instant healing like we would appreciate, this miracle will come in time through work and faith. Don't stop believing because your recovery is not complete. Keep asking, keep trusting, and keep believing that God is actively healing you still.

I can relate to the faith of the blind man in my own recovery. Looking back at my journey, I recognize what God has done for me. Through endless prayers said on my behalf and my personal pleas to God, I have been restored. God healed me, and I realize that I didn't do this on my own. Through God's hand, I was healed. Although not instant, God's healing was no less miraculous. As you consider your own healing process, praise God for His healing hand.

My prayer for you is that God will be near to you and strengthen you throughout your recovery. Jesus asked the blind man, "What do you want me to do for you?" Don't be afraid to ask the Lord for healing and for loving acceptance of the new you.

I leave you with this verse from Isaiah 40:31 (CEV): "But those who hope in the Lord will renew their strength; they will soar on wings like eagles; they will run and not grow weary, they will walk and not be faint." Hope is more than wishful thinking; it is the belief in a positive outcome toward a better future, even when circumstances are uncertain. The Bible says hope is a confident expectation of what God has promised, rooted in His faithfulness. Just as Jesus was faithful to honor the request of the blind man, Jesus has been and will be faithful to us.

CHAPTER 5

Life After TBI

The first year of intense recovery passed, and I started gradually reengaging with life. Maybe it seemed like the story was coming to an end, but then there was a change, a twist, and a new beginning. My doctor told me I would reach my peak of improvement within the first twelve months. I kept that thought in mind, believing I would be done improving by then. I am here to tell you that improvement and therapy have been my saving grace many times, even into my fifties.

I began learning different coping skills to navigate my life experiences. I used three resources: a list, a week at a glance, and a monthly calendar to keep life organized. Some of these resources I had before my accident, but now they became more important for organizing my life. I taught full-time and frequently referred to my lesson plan booklet, making it a familiar tool for managing my life as I had done prior to my TBI. This type of visual organizing is a continued comfort for me.

In the fall of 1999, I was preparing to go back to teaching. I opened my closet and was trying to decide what to wear. My mind drifted back to the day of the accident, the first day after Christmas break the previous year. It was usual for me to be sporting a new Christmas outfit on that first day back to school. Suddenly, I realized I couldn't remember what I had been wearing, and then it struck me that the entire day was missing from my memory.

Shortly after that revelation, I went back to my neurologist for a follow-up appointment and asked him about my memory loss. He explained how memories work. He told me that immediate memories are converted into short-term memories when we voluntarily go to sleep on the same day. However, because I had been put into a drug-induced coma on the day of my accident, that entire day had vanished for me. I do feel fortunate to have all my memories up until the day of the accident and beyond.

I have now learned that memory loss is a common consequence of traumatic brain injury, and it can affect both short-term and long-term memory. The severity and type of memory impairment depend on the location and extent of the brain damage. While some individuals experience lasting amnesia, others may only struggle with recalling recent events or learning new information.

You may also experience some type of memory loss, and it might be helpful to explore that and discuss it with your doctor. Here are some things I've learned about memory impairment that helped me understand my issues. You might have trouble remembering events that happened before or after the injury. You may find it difficult to form new memories after the injury or to recall recent events such as what you went to the store for. In some cases, people struggle to remember long-term events or general knowledge. All these issues depend on how severe the injury was, which part of the brain was affected, or the stage of recovery you're in. There are many other factors, strategies, and tools to help you cope with your specific memory loss. It's helpful to remember that recovery is generally a long-term process, and it's important to ask for the help and support you need along the way.

A few years of my recovery passed quickly, and I began thinking about how much I appreciated the care I had received at the rehab hospital. One day, Mike and I were near my rehabilitation hospital, so we stopped in. We took the elevator to the floor where I had been. I was so excited to see the staff, thinking they would be happy to see my progress. However, they recognized Mike from his frequent visits and praised him for how well he was doing.

We quickly realized they didn't recognize me because my hair had grown back and I was walking pretty well by then. Mike quickly cleared up their confusion and pointed out that I had been the patient some years earlier. We all laughed about the mix-up, and they eagerly congratulated me on my progress. I now realize that without their help and God's support, I wouldn't have been able to walk into that hospital with the pride I felt that day.

Recovery from a TBI is a tough journey for every survivor. You might be at a stage of achievement or a stage of struggle. Your recovery may not look like what you had hoped for, or you might feel relieved because you've had some success. I compare this seesaw process to a lesson I taught my kindergarten students about the life cycle of a butterfly. First is the egg, which symbolizes the accident as a beginning. Then there is the caterpillar, which represents the hospital stay as a more intense experience where we begin to change and grow. And finally, the beautiful butterfly emerges, which symbolizes the new you.

God doesn't care about clocks or calendars. He knows the right time. I believe my steps are already in motion; I just need to catch up with God's plan for me.

I returned to teaching kindergarten part-time in the 1999–2000 school year. I can rejoice in the fact that I secured a job and taught for a year, receiving many positive comments. I enjoyed the support from the beautiful families, those precious children, and my colleagues. I wish I had felt more accomplished, but I was comparing myself to the old me and remembering a more capable teacher. I was pleased to know that even this school had prayed for my safe recovery in 1998.

As I tried to reenter teaching, I faced a variety of challenges— especially bulletin boards since I didn't feel balanced when I climbed the ladder. Skipping and hopping were also difficult. I could give directions to the children, but I couldn't model the actions the way I used to. I thought that being back in my profession, especially with part-time work, would make me feel revitalized, but instead, I was exhausted by Wednesday each week.

Part-time didn't feel like half the workload. I did things more slowly and cautiously. I believed teaching was natural for me, but the large and small motor skills I had previously used were now problematic. I realized I needed to make a change. I really enjoyed teaching and flourished in the profession, but

I wasn't meeting my own expectations. I began to wonder why I ended up in this situation with the car accident. Was this God's plan for me all along, or was the plan to save me through it all and alter my path?

By March 2000, I decided I wouldn't go back to teaching kindergarten the following year. I felt mental relief for having made that decision. At the same time, I was already thinking about my next step.

I wanted to stay in the education field and use my passion and expertise for children. The next step in my career was early childhood family education. I completed the courses to add parent education to my teaching license. I started working with parents and their young children from birth to age three. Each class met weekly or biweekly to explore, learn, and grow through play, classroom activities, and meaningful discussions. I love that I can now observe children develop, be a friendly observer, and serve as a reliable resource for parents. That role is a great fit for me, utilizing my skills and fulfilling my passion by keeping my brain stimulated at a comfortable pace.

You might also need to evaluate your career path. If parts of your past career no longer fit your needs or make you feel successful, I encourage you to step back and consider your skills and interests. Find a place where you can feel happy and productive, and give yourself a break to recognize the new person you have become.

For Mike and me, my TBI and other challenging circumstances in both our lives were hard on our marriage. Looking back, I realize that at the time, my attention and focus on various issues had changed. Our ability to support each other shifted, and we were approaching life from two different perspectives. I give myself grace because my TBI occurred when we were both twenty-six, but throughout life, people always change and grow. Missing the team approach led to our divorce after more than fifteen years.

We TBI survivors and our partners may struggle to connect with each other. When the other person experiences stress, we might find it harder to focus on supporting our partner like we used to. Some parts of our personality might have changed and may never fully return to what they once were. Traits like patience, compassion, intuition, and empathy may be lacking at times.

You might find this type of challenge occurring in your life as you go through your own recovery, focus, and reactions. I strongly suggest that you seek resources that can help you discover ways to reinvent yourselves as a team and rebuild a healthy relationship.

God in the Midst of TBI – When God Remains with You

The following verse offers encouragement as you open new doors and explore new ways to trust that God will continue to help you grow: "So neither the one who plants nor the one who waters is anything, but only God, who makes things grow" (1 Cor. 3:7 CEV). It's comforting to read those words and reflect on the hand of God upon us, providing what we need to grow and flourish.

It has now been twenty-seven years since my accident. As long as I can remember, I have always felt busy. I used to have so many things going on—school, friends, work, sports, several jobs at once—and I was able to keep it balanced. I was a high-functioning person. Since my accident, I have felt busy and wake up some days without a clean slate from the previous day.

Sometimes I find it helpful to think about the pros and cons of my life at this moment. I feel fortunate to be a mom. I feel a connection with my pets. I enjoy my Cavapoo support dog, Sheena, who greets me at the door. Her joy at seeing me never ends. I love that she can also sense when I need comfort and support. My outdoor cats delight me. They keep my yard free of rodents and often present them at my doorstep.

Along with many positives, there are still things I reflect on that I cannot do. I can't swim well, I can't run smoothly, I have foot pain, and I wear a brace on the hyperextension of my right knee. I am still here and pleased with how my life is evolving. I am thankful for all I *can* do. My switch to left-hand dominance after my accident has been successful. I can take my dog and cats who join us for frequent walks, bike using my recumbent assist bike, work in my yard, do yoga, manage my household, teach, and maintain many friendships. I am an author, at least after this book is published. I have a strong social group and have contributed to the development of many support groups. Most importantly, I have a deep faith in God who sustains me.

As I reflect on my journey after the TBI, I am thankful for many things, and I can see God's hand in my recovery. I deeply appreciate the first responder who took care of me immediately after the accident. I am grateful to my family and friends who constantly make me feel secure and loved. I was fortunate to be healthy at the time of my accident.

My strong temperament has given me the drive to succeed at whatever challenge has come my way. I am proud to say that I have become increasingly more independent over the past decade. I am strong and a bit spirited, and my family wondered if this personality trait would change. Thankfully, it has become my advantage, and this characteristic has grown even stronger.

Now in my fifties, I realize that this TBI is a permanent part of my life that sometimes rears its ugly head. I want to share a recent example. I share this incident to give you permission to forgive yourself and say you're sorry if something similar happens to you. Just yesterday, after twenty-seven years of living with my TBI, I did something I'm not proud of. I had a phone call with someone I love, and their comment triggered a verbal reaction that isn't characteristic of me. Within seconds, I was shocked at my own response and asked for forgiveness. That may happen to you when your feelings get trapped inside and you are pushed down on your emotional survival ladder.

It's hard to know when your patience or good sense will spill over. I found this to be more common during the first couple years of my recovery. However, yesterday, the extra layer of tension was just too much and ended in a bust. I believe that this type of reaction is not that uncommon, but the key to avoiding the negative impulse is to listen more loudly than you talk. That means to take notice, take a breath, and then speak.

Every survivor heals differently and goes through different stages at different times. Arm yourself with coping tools, take naps when needed, and spend time with pets if that helps. Ask for help to manage the things you cannot handle or that overwhelm you, and most importantly, give yourself permission to love the new person you are becoming.

Know that God will meet you exactly where you are. He can handle your disappointments and will guide you compassionately toward a new life filled with inner confidence, joy, and self-love.

As you continue your journey with TBI, remember Psalm 37:23–24 (NIV): "The Lord makes firm the steps of the one who delights in Him; though he may stumble, he will not fall, for the Lord upholds him with His hand." He is holding you up. He will remain with you. He has not gone anywhere, and He will not leave you. Place your trust in Him, and He will not let you down.

Thank you for sharing this journey with me. I hope that what I shared provides reassurance through my experiences and will serve as a resource to you as you navigate your own recovery. I believe that God has all our lives planned out, and we need to trust Him. He knows all your days and is with you in them all.

I'll leave you with this encouragement: Who you are right now and who you aspire to be in the future are within reach. Go get it and make it happen. I know you can.

And I'll leave you with this prayer:

> You made me perfect in Your eyes. Help me continue to grow and change in ways that show up physically, emotionally, and spiritually. I am constantly changing and adapting to how You are perfectly healing and shaping me.

Sandra's Story
as a TBI Caregiver

CHAPTER 6
The Initial Shock

A single phone call can change your life. In the early hours of January 1, 2003, I received a call that changed my life. Before that call, my family felt optimistic about our recent transition from rural life to a small city. We were settling into a new routine filled with bright possibilities and enjoying a season of calm. That phone call threw me and my family into deep water, and we had to swim.

My husband and I were high school sweethearts who grew up in rural America, married two years after graduation, and grew into adulthood together. We loved the country life and wanted it for our children, so we chose to stay. We welcomed our babies—a daughter followed fourteen months later by a son named Tim, and then four years later a second son as the whirlwind of raising kids engulfed us. Twelve years flew by in a blink, and we entered the phase of sporting events and music concerts, toting a video camera to capture each moment. Then we added a baby carrier and a diaper bag as we welcomed a fourth child—a third son—into our family. Life was a joyful blur.

After forty-nine years in small-town America, our careers took us to a medium-sized city about two and a half hours away. Most of our children had gone in various directions for college and work, but our oldest son, Tim, remained on the farm where he had been raised. When we moved out and he moved in, he stated firmly, "I am never moving again."

Our daughter got married and then made us proud, first-time grandparents. Our middle son worked in a nearby town, while our fourth-grade youngest son moved with us to the city. Life in our new surroundings was exciting, yet we kept in touch and gathered often.

My story as the mother of a victim of traumatic brain injury (TBI) begins on New Year's Eve 2002. My husband and I, along with our youngest son who was in seventh grade, were having our own New Year's Eve party. We enjoyed our favorite snacks and watched two of our favorite movies, with the plan to see the ball drop in New York City. It was around 10:30 p.m., and our eyes grew heavy as we snuggled together on the sofa.

"Should we call it a night?" I asked, looking at their sleepy faces. I put away the treats, the hats, and the whistles, and said, "We can say hello to the New Year in the morning." We all laughed and happily went to bed.

The telephone jolted us out of a deep sleep in the early morning hours of New Year's Day. My husband answered the phone, and a chill ran down my spine when I heard the voice of an old friend. There was an urgency in his voice as he spoke. "I heard that there was an accident near your old place. I heard Tim was involved." He paused and added, "It sounds bad. I'll drive over there and let you know."

We were up, awake, and aware as adrenaline rushed through our veins. The last ten years flashed through my mind as I recalled how Tim's rebellious teen years had extended into his twenties. He had become a skilled backhoe operator who built roads, worked hard, and earned money. He was part of the pit crew for a friend with a race car, and he remained, as he always had been, a jovial social magnet, generous with his time and resources.

While Tim maintained an active social life, he was an active and dynamic part of our family, even though he wasn't always as pleasant with us as he was with his friends. When he attended family events in his twenties, he often came across as edgy, pushing back against our questions or comments, sleeping through our social times together, and showing disrespect for family plans. We watched and waited, hoping Tim would find his way back to a more peaceful life.

After hanging up the phone, my husband and I were filled with fear. My reaction was to prepare, though I had no idea what I was preparing for. I went to our bedroom, grabbed a small suitcase, and packed a change of clothes for all three of us. I hadn't woken our youngest son yet. With our hearts pounding and our senses heightened, we waited—five minutes, ten minutes, fifteen minutes. Finally, the phone rang. My husband grabbed it and said, "Yes."

I heard a voice on the other end of the line while I watched my husband tense up. He tilted the phone so I could hear better. The person on the call said she was from the local hospital near our small town. She spoke slowly and clearly. She asked if Tim was our son. Next, she said without pausing, "You need to come here immediately."

We asked, "Is he okay?" She did not answer. She said again, "Please come."

We hung up the phone, and without hesitation, I woke our youngest son. I said, "There's been an accident. Get up and get dressed. We have to go."

I grabbed the small bag I had packed along with a blanket and pillow for our son. As we put on our coats, my husband said, "I should grab that bag phone." He picked up the phone, and the three of us got into the truck.

As we opened the garage door and looked out, we realized that we hadn't checked the weather. Snow swirled around the truck as we backed out of the garage. The outside temperature gauge kept dropping until it reached minus 10 degrees. We turned on the radio to a local station and heard, "Roads will be slick, visibility diminished. Snow will accumulate through the night." We looked at each other, nodded, and drove on.

We navigated through the neighborhood streets and county roads and then entered the freeway. We understood that under favorable road conditions, this trip should take about two hours. We drove on in tense silence. Large flakes of wet snow stuck to the windshield as the wipers swished back and forth and the wind howled all around us.

We were jarred from our silence as the bag phone rang. My husband clumsily pulled the phone out of the bag and blurted, "Hello." A voice of steel cut through the air, asking if we were the parents of Tim. With an affirmative answer, the voice went on. "Your son is being airlifted to the nearest level one trauma center. Please do not stop here; go directly to MeritCare." There was a pause, and then the voice continued, "Do you have other immediate family?"

My husband said, "Yes, we do."

The voice said, "You should call them." They said goodbye.

My husband laid the phone on the console between us. We remained silent. My mind raced with questions that had no answers. We drove on, cocooned in an empty void, realizing that the distance we now needed to cover would be at least two hours longer. What we found had no face, nothing we could examine or consider, only the black hole of nothingness. There was no experience we had encountered before that could provide context for the reality we were about to face.

We called our daughter, her new husband, and our middle son to deliver the message. "There has been an accident, and Tim is being airlifted to MeritCare." They both replied that they would be on their way as soon as possible.

The snow kept falling, and silence engulfed us. We had no words and no tears, only the terror of what lay ahead.

Finally, I looked at my husband and said, "You know, if they are airlifting him, doesn't that mean he is still alive?"

He looked at me without comment, and we drove on.

As a woman who loves the Lord, I would like to say that we prayed throughout the entire drive to MeritCare, but we didn't. When fear took over, we focused entirely on the immediate urgency of getting to our son. Whatever his condition, whatever the problem, and whatever happened next, we needed to be there.

Reflecting on that call and the hours that followed, I realize that God was carrying us. Even though we were focused on ourselves, our drive, and our children, He was focused on us. He

71

guided our thoughts and our reactions, keeping us calm enough to handle the phone calls and the unknown. He restrained panic but allowed fear. He carried us every step of that night and brought us safely to the hospital where we would find our son.

People often believe they cannot handle sudden trauma. An accident, an illness, or an unexpected death all come without warning. The reality is that you can manage it because, whether you realize it or not, God is there to carry you.

The snow continued to swirl around us, but the roads were not slippery. We stayed behind the heavy-load trucks whenever possible to block the wind, and the hours ticked on. We remained enveloped in silence, each lost in our thoughts, with our youngest son asleep in the back seat of the truck.

Finally, we turned off the freeway and headed toward the hospital. We parked quickly and walked into the emergency entrance. My body tensed as two medical personnel greeted us. We identified ourselves as Tim's family and were led into a curtained corridor.

The nurse stopped at a curtain and pulled it back to reveal a body lying on a gurney. A respirator was positioned nearby with tubes extending into Tim's mouth. The machine emitted a swooshing, rhythmic sound. A bag of IV fluid hung beside the gurney, its liquid flowing into our son's arm.

Tim remained completely still, a white cloth draped over his torso. His muscular arms lay bare, covered in abrasions crusted with dirt, gravel, and dried blood. I touched his hand that lay limp at his side and smoothed his fingers. I looked at his face, tan from the sun, his chiseled cheekbones, and his deep-set eyes closed and silent. I assured him that we were present. This was the strongest, toughest young man I knew—my son who pushed the limits of everything and struggled to give me a hug. He now was motionless. My tears were close, yet they did not spill out.

We three stood around him as our middle son entered the room. These two brothers were buddies and knew many of each other's secrets. The anguish on my middle son's face as he looked at his big brother overwhelmed my emotions, and tears rolled down my cheeks, dropping to the floor as we hugged and cried together.

I became aware that a new presence was in the room. A doctor in a white coat and a steady voice introduced himself as a neurosurgeon. I looked at him in all my innocence and said, "He will be okay, right?"

He looked back at me, his voice grave. "Mrs. Fabian, your son is in critical condition. We won't know the outcome for some time." He added sternly, "He had been drinking and that does not help this situation. I just want you to know that."

He turned toward my husband. "We will want you to sign a release; we need to put a probe in his skull to relieve the pressure."

My husband went to the desk to sign the document, and Tim was rolled away while we were escorted to a waiting area. Sitting in the waiting room, my voice silent and my mind in a fog, I heard the doctor's words: "critical condition."

A nurse gently pushed open the door, gesturing to my husband. "There is a call for you," she said softly. After a few minutes, my husband returned to the waiting room and shared that one of the local first responders had called to check on Tim. He provided us with one piece of the puzzle regarding what had happened that night. He shared that Tim had been a passenger in a friend's vehicle. They had been at a bar in town and were on their way to Tim's house in the country. As they rounded a curve in the road, the vehicle left the road and flew into a grove of trees. The passenger side of the vehicle hit several trees multiple times. The driver was not seriously injured. Another car that was following them contacted the first responders.

The caller added, "We were really scared. Tim stopped breathing a few times at the scene, and we thought we were going to lose him right there. We thought we would have to call you guys and say we lost Tim." Small towns can be like one big family where everyone knows and cares about each other.

Sudden trauma impacts people in different and multiple ways. Reactions manifest in emotional, physical, and behavioral waves. Each person will respond differently, and there is no one correct path. These reactions are often normal and expected as the body and mind grapple with the impact of a deeply distressing experience. Understanding these reactions is crucial for individuals navigating the aftermath of trauma and seeking appropriate support.

Here are some common immediate reactions:

- *Fight, Flight, or Freeze:* These are instinctive responses to perceived danger that involve either confronting the threat, escaping from it, or becoming immobile. They are triggered by the body's stress response, which releases adrenaline and prepares the body for action.
- *Shock and Disbelief:* Feeling numb, detached, or unable to fully process the event is a typical initial reaction. This can serve as a coping mechanism while the brain attempts to absorb the overwhelming information.

- *Intense Emotions:* A wide range of emotions can emerge, including fear, anxiety, anger, sadness, guilt, and shame. They may be intense and fluctuate significantly in the immediate aftermath.
- *Physical Symptoms:* The body may experience various physical reactions, including an increased heart rate, difficulty sleeping, changes in appetite, headaches, and muscle tension.
- *Memory Problems:* Difficulty concentrating, memory lapses, and flashbacks are common responses as the brain struggles to process the traumatic experience.
- *Social Withdrawal:* Some individuals might withdraw from social interactions, feeling overwhelmed or unable to handle the emotional demands of relationships.

It is good to recognize normal reactions and embrace them to cope with a new reality. My reaction to this experience is different from even members of my own family, and I realize there is no right or wrong way; there is your way. I believe it is helpful to notice that friends and family around you also have a response. These responses can be supportive, uncomfortable, empathetic, sympathetic, and even judgmental. Sometimes it helps to hear from people, and sometimes you wish they would just go away.

God in the Midst of TBI – When God Carries You

One thing I know without question is that the comfort of our Lord is the comfort that sustains me. The silent whisper, a song that awakens my thoughts, random words spoken, and dreams that come from nowhere are the messages I try to recognize. I believe they are not luck or coincidence. I believe they are sent by the hand of God.

Below are two messages that have lingered in my consciousness since that first night. They have remained with me for the past twenty-two years, and I believe they are as true today as they were on that night.

The first message is from Proverbs 3:5, which says, "Trust in the LORD with all your heart, and do not rely on your own understanding." Trusting that the Lord is in charge and surrendering control to His will is a difficult and seemingly impossible task. Those words brought me comfort that night and in the days that followed. I repeated them over and over as Jesus's loving arms enveloped me. Saying the words *I trust you, Jesus* even if you don't mean them at first can and will bring you peace.

When panic and fear overwhelm you, turn to Jesus. He doesn't care whether you know Him well or haven't talked in a while. He is waiting and wanting to hear from you. The words do not matter; He is present with you, and all you have to do is turn to Him.

Much about your life will come into question the moment trauma enters your world. The bottom will feel like it's dropping out, and everything that once seemed stable and certain in your life will collapse with you. If you know Jesus, even your faith can feel shaken and unstable as questions flood your mind about how God could allow something like this to happen. And if you don't know Jesus when something like this occurs, let me encourage you to consider this a catalyst for faith.

Our faith journey while caring for someone with TBI has its ups and downs, but this verse reminds me that we can only see so far, while the Lord sees farther than we do. You might not feel capable, but as someone who's on the other side of their journey through TBI, I know that you can. Trust the Lord with all your heart, and leave the rest to Him.

The second message is the song "You'll Never Walk Alone," sung first by Frank Sinatra in 1945 and later by Elvis Presley in 1967. The words permeated my thoughts as a spiritual message. Listen to that song and look up those lyrics online. They will speak to you as you walk through your tragedy, as you keep walking through every storm, not alone but with your Father God.

Through this song, God said to me, "You will never walk alone." His promise in those words provided the reassurance I needed that night. Our God carries us when we need it and speaks to us where and when we can hear Him. We may never be fully prepared to receive the call that changes our lives and the lives of those we love. But God will be with you through it all. If you allow Him, He will carry you, even when you are unaware, gently holding you up and faithfully caring for your heart and soul as you learn to care for your loved one with TBI.

Our God is with us, especially during the storms of life. I encourage you to listen for the voice of God, even when the voices of fear threaten to overwhelm you. He is speaking to you, comforting, guiding, directing, and caring, even when it's hard to hear. He is for you and will be with you. Our God carries us when we need Him and speaks to us where and when we can hear Him.

CHAPTER 7

Waiting in the ICU

It was Wednesday, January 1, 2003—a new year as the crisp winter sunlight brightened the room. We began the day after our introduction to traumatic brain injury.

We had been moved from the waiting room near the emergency area to a waiting room in the intensive care unit (ICU). The television droned on as we sat in silence.

At some point during those early morning hours, the neurosurgeon who had taken Tim for the probe placement pushed open the door. He reached out to shake our hands and sat in a chair beside the sofa, quietly stating, "We will watch the pressure for increased swelling on his brain."

He paused, seemingly to allow his words to sink in, and then continued. "He is in a medically induced coma at this point so he remains still and his brain can heal. He has no broken bones, and that is good. We will continue to support his neck with a cervical collar, just in case there is a neck or spinal injury we aren't aware of. Now we watch and hope that the swelling goes down. There is nothing to do but wait."

We were allowed to enter Tim's room, two at a time, for short periods. The swoosh of the ventilator pushing air into his lungs, the fluid dripping into his veins, the catheter draining his bladder, and the banks of blinking monitors reminded us of where we were. He was covered with a crisp white sheet and lay perfectly still.

"We will wait" hung heavy in my consciousness. I was walking, talking, asking questions, and trying to comfort and support the rest of my family, but I felt empty. I could not comprehend that our journey was just beginning. My only thoughts were on how we could cope with the immediate situation and how long we would wait.

Our daughter and her family arrived. They had driven over five hours in the cold, snowy, winter weather. Tim and his sister were a little more than a year apart in age, and during their preschool and early elementary years, they were playmates and best friends. They carved out secret forts in the woods, built treehouses, and learned to ride their bikes. They worked together on animal chores, spent hours creating theatrical events (we were the audience), and were partners in mischief. They played dress-up, played with matchbox cars, attended ballet class, and played baseball. When reminiscing about those early years, Tim often remarked, "Whatever my sister did as a child, I did too."

In high school and early adulthood, the two of them took different paths in their choices and social activities, which caused them to grow apart. Yet now, when her brother was in trouble, she set aside all that and came without hesitation to support him.

Our group of four grew to seven. Our one-year-old granddaughter was a bright presence as she played on the floor in the waiting room. The seven of us took turns entering Tim's room to sit for a while as our minds began to awaken to the fact that it was a new day and a new year, and that life continued. We started making lists. We needed to call Grandma and Grandpa so they didn't hear the news from someone else. My husband and I needed to reach out to our siblings and close friends. Our adult children began to think about who would want to know as we delegated who would do what. We needed to handle Tim's home, his work, and his bills. We needed to enact a power of attorney on his behalf so we could access his bank accounts and try to keep his life going.

"What do we say when we call?" our daughter asked.

"The message is that we don't know anything and no visitors are allowed right now," her dad answered.

The calling began as more thoughts filtered through our minds. The following day would be Thursday, January 2, the first day of school after a two-week Christmas break, and our youngest son was here in the hospital with us. We needed to call our pastor to step down from our commitments and, more importantly, ask for prayers. I needed to call my work and request immediate flexibility. My husband, who was self-employed, had to make arrangements with his business partner to cover his projects.

What no one tells you about a sudden traumatic incident is all the ways that irrevocably change the moment you receive that call. Not only was our son's life forever altered, but our lives changed in the blink of an eye as well. As we continued to make calls and sort out the details of work, school, and our other obligations, we began to realize it would be a long time before we returned to anything closely resembling the life we once knew.

Tim's pastor in the small town where he lived called us to say he had already heard and was on his way. As the word spread that first day, we learned that prayer chains had started all across the state and beyond. People reached out to each other and linked prayers from one church to another. We could feel the warmth of caring and the love of God, and we were so thankful.

Wednesday, Thursday, and Friday all blurred together as we moved into the family housing provided by the hospital. My husband and I tried to stay in Tim's room, seated beside his bed, watching him in a blank fog until finally a nurse came in and said gently, "You need to get some rest; we will let you know if there is any change." We were hesitant but exhausted as we left his room and walked across the street to our housing and to bed that Friday night.

Sometime during the night, the beeper we had been given jolted us out of a fitful sleep. We called the ICU and identified ourselves. The voice on the other end stated with urgency, "Please come immediately." We put on some clothes, slipped on our shoes, and grabbed our coats as my mind plunged into a blank of confusion and terror all over again.

We entered Tim's room where a team of medical personnel was gathered. We were told that Tim's oxygen level and heart rate had dropped dangerously low and that he had been given some medication to stabilize him. We were horrified as it became clear that we could still lose our son. We waited a while beside his still body, listening to the swoosh of the ventilator and watching the lights and tubes, when a doctor came in and assured us he was stable for now.

"I'm going to take a walk," I said, and began to wander down the hallway, putting one foot in front of the other as I passed rooms filled with beeping lights, whooshing ventilators, and tubes hanging everywhere. As I rounded the corner, a ray of colored light shimmered on the floor of the hallway. Two heavy wooden doors were open, welcoming me to enter the hospital chapel. A row of wooden pews hugged either side of a short, carpeted aisle, guiding me forward as tears ran down my cheeks and dropped to the floor. The aisle led to an altar that flickered with candlelight, and above it, a huge white cross hung freely from the ceiling. Behind the cross, a wall was alive with glistening colored glass made bright by the early morning winter sunlight behind it.

I fell to my knees at the altar rail and wept. I think I said aloud, "We are in real trouble, Father." In that moment, I felt a peace fall upon me; I did not know what would happen next, but I did know I was not alone, my family was not alone, and my son was not alone. I stayed a little while longer, soaking in the peace before returning to the ICU, feeling a renewed sense of strength.

There are times when our burden is so heavy and the fear and grief so raw that we believe we cannot bear it. Jesus knows us, sees us, and remains near to help carry our burden. "I trust you, Jesus," I repeated again and again until I could breathe once more.

"Be still and know that I am God" (Ps. 46:10 NIV).

This simple verse reminds me to stay aware and sense the small voice deep within—the voice that says, "It will be okay. I've got you." In the most difficult times of life, God is telling us to be quiet with Him and know that He is with us and is always in charge. The hardest thing to do is submit to God, be still, and listen, trusting Him in all things. Indeed, He is God. He knows all, sees all, and is in control of all things.

In Luke 22:41–43, Jesus was desperate to know that His Father was still with Him. Jesus walked away from His disciples to be alone with His Father. These verses remind us that even Jesus wanted His burden lifted, but He said, "Not my will, but yours be done" (Luke 22:42 NIV). God's will can be visible to us, but more often it is invisible. His comfort is found in trust. "I trust you, Jesus." I encourage you to say that until you mean it.

The following morning was Saturday, January 4. Four days after the accident, we gathered for a family meeting with the neurosurgeon and the neuropsychologist. My husband and I sat at the table, surrounded by our middle son, our youngest son, our daughter, our son-in-law, and our granddaughter. The two doctors, their faces solemn, smiled with reservation, sat down, shook our hands, and began.

The surgeon had a matter-of-fact tone. "Tim's condition remains critical. I want you to know that should the pressure increase any more, we will have to open his skull to relieve it. The episode that happened last night may happen again as swelling like this pushes on the brain stem and interferes with the autonomic, automatic system that controls heart rate and breathing." He paused as we all caught our breath and then continued. "He will stay in a medically induced coma for at least one more week and then be reassessed. You need to stay close if you can."

I asked the neuropsychologist about my son's injury. He said, "Well, if you took a bowl of oatmeal and threw it at the wall, picked up the pieces and threw it again, and then picked up those pieces and threw it once more, that is what happened to your son's brain."

I didn't ask any more questions as tears welled up in my eyes. *Dear God, please help us.*

The neuropsychologist paused a moment and added, "The brain has amazing abilities to rewire itself. There are stages of recovery. The early stages usually begin with no response, then involuntary movement, and then inconsistent responses. There are later stages of confusion and return of function. Each person's recovery trajectory and rehabilitation are different. For now, we need you to describe Tim for us." He explained that if Tim began to wake up, it was important for the staff to recognize any common behaviors or personality traits. He said, "Tell me about his personality and how he interacted with you. What did he like or dislike, what kind of music or books did he like, what were his hobbies?"

We described his happy-go-lucky, risk-taking personality, his deep-set blue eyes that could stare a hole through you, his love for fun and friends, and even his loyalty to our family. We talked about his toughness and his ability to feel no pain. We mentioned that he could be really crabby and bullheaded, yet he could also be a big teddy bear depending on the day and the situation.

The neuropsychologist explained to us that Tim could hear us even though his eyes were closed and he was unresponsive. He encouraged us to talk to him and to each other in his presence. He mentioned that reading something calm and gentle is beneficial. He also cautioned us not to talk about him, not to raise our voices, and not to argue while in the room. Lastly, he stated that we can and should touch him; his senses of hearing, touch, and smell were active and should be stimulated.

It had only been a few days, but our family had instinctively begun a cycle of sitting by his side, talking to him, and holding his hand. After the meeting, we all agreed that someone from our immediate family would stay with him continuously. My husband, our daughter, our middle son, and I worked together to create a calendar based on who could take time off work and when.

It was Sunday, January 5, and we needed to focus on our youngest son in seventh grade who had become very quiet during the last few days. He sat with us in the waiting room but did not want to visit Tim's room. We worried about him and thought it was best for him to get back to school. He had already missed the first two days of the spring semester. We knew his world had been turned upside down in an instant.

He was born into a family of five—my husband, myself, and three older siblings who watched over him like hawks. He was our family treasure. His big brother Tim loved to have him tag along and showed him off to his friends. Now, his big, strong brother was missing, replaced by silence and tears, heavy words and hospitals, beepers and meetings. We talked with him about going back home to school, and he agreed. We made arrangements with extended family to help him get back into some kind of familiar routine. We called the school administration and asked that the staff be alerted to his new reality and offer any necessary support.

We did what we could to support him and provide some sense of normalcy. We arranged for a tutor to check in with him at school and be available to help with his homework. However, we learned much later that he had avoided any interaction at school about what had happened to our family over that Christmas break. It was many years later that we realized how devastating this experience was for him. As an adult, he shared that he had been approached by a couple of teachers and a counselor but had not disclosed anything. He had suppressed his feelings and fear and later said, "I was just waiting for life to return to normal." His routine had shifted to five days of school and weekends spent traveling three hours to the hospital and back. He had gone through the motions of life, but it was not normal.

On the late afternoon of Sunday, January 5, my husband drove home to make work arrangements and drop off our youngest son with extended family. I stayed at the hospital to begin the first couple of days of our vigil. Our daughter and family left on the five-hour trek across the state, while our middle son drove home to make his own arrangements.

The days began to fly by as our family members took turns sitting by Tim's side day and night, day after day. Visitors started arriving, regardless of whether they could see Tim or not. Among the first were Grandma and Grandpa. My dad and my husband's mom were the two grandparents present at that time. Our families were friends, and we had all lived in the same small town.

Grandma was 5 feet tall and had a round waistline and a stern voice. She loved gathering her family and prioritized having fun together. Having raised seven children, she now also enjoyed seventeen grandchildren. She loved to bake, and as her grandchildren grew up and went off to college, she gifted them a covered tin box filled with all their favorite cookies. She said, "Eat these up, bring the tin back, and I will refill it." Tim, who adored Grandma's cookies, brought the tin box back for a refill several times.

Grandpa lived right across the street from the school, and our children often stopped by to see him. He was a retired farmer who went to cattle auctions "just to keep his mind sharp" and loved a good game of euchre. His twinkling deep-brown eyes, fun-loving personality, and big smile lit up a room. Grandpa, Tim, and our middle son went on fishing trips to Canada, played golf together in the summer, and ice fished during the winter months. Tim often said that Grandpa was his best friend. As Tim grew into his twenties, Grandpa often told him, "If you are in town at the bar, don't drive. Just walk over to my place and go home in the morning." Tim had taken that advice many times.

As Grandma and Grandpa arrived and before they entered Tim's room, we talked with them about what had happened and what they would see. Both were seasoned by many difficult life events, but it was dreadful to see their faces as we walked into Tim's darkened room filled with his quiet body and the sights and sounds of life support. The proper sequence of the oldest among us failing first and the youngest carrying forward our legacy was in jeopardy at that point. Life was turned upside down for all of us.

Our parents each visited Tim in the ICU only once, and we never encouraged them to come again. We updated them over the phone, and that was enough information for them. I believe they, just like our youngest son, were waiting for life to return to normal.

One afternoon as my daughter and I sat together chatting at Tim's bedside, she said, "Don't you think Tim would enjoy a foot massage?" We agreed, pulled the sheet off his feet, applied lotion to our hands, and each took a foot and began gently rubbing in the lotion. We laughed as we entertained the thought that if he suddenly awoke, he would sit up, stare at us with those deep blue eyes, and say, "What the . . . are you guys doing?"

We were chuckling and reminiscing when a nurse entered. "What are you doing?" she asked. "Stop rubbing his feet," she said. "The feet are filled with nerve endings that would overstimulate his brain. Right now we need his brain to rest and heal." We stopped, covered up his feet, and sat down, chuckling as we thought about those piercing eyes of his. "It's a good thing he didn't wake up," my daughter quipped.

The family of the driver involved in the accident came to see us. His parents and brother sat with us, discussing the stitches their son and brother had received that night. At that moment, I realized I needed to step out of the room to calm myself. I was struck by the stark differences between the injuries of these two young men. Both were at fault for drinking and getting on the road, but it was my son who lay in the bed, unable to breathe on his own.

Many of Tim's friends and coworkers visited the ICU. Some of them, we knew, had been at the scene the night of the accident. They were horrified when they saw him, and our hearts ached for them. We didn't ask any questions, and they didn't offer any answers. We just sat there knowing there was more to the story. We also knew that although our lives and our son's life were completely changed, it had been an accident—an unintentional, terrible accident.

We felt overwhelmed by the daily mail filled with cards and messages of love and support. Several times, we received boxes brimming with goodies for all of us. We enjoyed and appreciated those bright moments that provided us a little reprieve as we discovered the contents inside.

Sometime toward the beginning of the third week, a social worker came in to sit with me. She suggested that we open a CaringBridge on the Internet so family and friends could hear directly from us and respond with messages that we could read immediately. I received instructions on how to create and manage the site. I began making daily entries on CaringBridge, and we were humbled by the support and prayers that flowed from the site.

Our CaringBridge received nearly a thousand messages from mid-January until mid-April 2003. Each message was loving, supportive, and meaningful. Here are a few shortened examples:

> "Prayers are with you."
> "Timmy, you are strong. May God strengthen you each day."
> "The CaringBridge was passed on to me. Our entire church is praying."
> "Thanks for keeping us updated."
> "Every step forward is progress. Hang in there."
> "Just read the morning entry. Don't give up."
> "Every day you are on our minds and in our hearts. We love you."

It meant so much to us when people reached out with their support. Wherever you are on your journey with sudden trauma, don't be afraid to reach out and accept the love and support of those around you. There is a palpable energy that flows through those words and prayers. When you feel your hope fading and your confusion growing, let your guard down and allow someone to compliment your courage. You will feel better, and so will they.

The emergency events related to Tim's breathing ceased toward the end of the third week of January, prompting the decision to try to wean him off the ventilator. They would extubate—remove his breathing tube—and hope he would begin to breathe on his own. They attempted that, but it was unsuccessful. He did not take a breath and was reintubated.

Dear God, he cannot breathe, I thought. The horror was too unimaginable.

Our panic grew as weaning him from the ventilator was attempted a second and third time without success. We were informed that he was going to surgery for a tracheotomy (trach) and the addition of a feeding tube. We were told that the trach procedure, which involves moving the tubing from his mouth directly into his trachea, would be more comfortable, and the feeding tube would provide him with necessary nourishment. I understood that both of those procedures indicated a longer-term situation.

Dear God, my son cannot breathe on his own. My mind again fixed on that reality. The outlook for his recovery darkened. He could not breathe on his own, he was not waking up, and our journey was uncertain. We had no choice but to walk by faith and not by sight.

The medical staff applauded and encouraged our family's vigil of sitting with him, reading to him, talking to him, and touching him, as we stayed by his side day and night. The power of prayer and the love and support of family and friends sustained us during those early days.

At the beginning of the last week of January, we were told his condition was stable with the trach and feeding tube in place. The social worker came in to gently initiate the discussion about the next steps. Tim needed to be moved out of ICU, and the medical staff had started looking for a rehabilitation hospital that would accept a patient with a tracheotomy on a ventilator who required specialized nursing care. We were about to begin a new chapter on our TBI journey as we waited for instructions.

God in the Midst of TBI – When God Holds You

I don't know where you are on your journey with TBI. You might be at the beginning like I was, wondering if those you care about will ever recover and feeling filled with uncertainty, anxiety, and fear about the possibilities ahead of you. You could be past those initial moments and farther along, gradually putting the pieces of your life back together. Regardless of your current stage, I want to encourage you with this truth: God is here with you and is holding you even now.

I know that not only from my experience but also from what God's Word tells us about how He cares for us when the unimaginable happens. The Bible is filled with words that strengthen, support, and comfort us. These words from the Psalms are offered to apply to your own situation. In the darkest of times, know that God is your refuge.

God is our refuge and strength, a helper who is always found in times of trouble. Therefore we will not be afraid though the earth trembles and the mountains topple into the depths of the seas.

—Ps. 46:1–2

For He will give his angels orders concerning you, to protect you in all your ways. They will support you with their hands so that you will not strike your foot against a stone.

—Ps. 91:11–12

Notice what the psalmist declares in the middle of his trial, "a helper who is always found in times of trouble." That echoes the reminder from the author of Hebrews in Hebrews 13:5–6 where he says that God promises to never leave or forsake us. He is present with you, even now, to be your refuge and your strength. The promise here isn't that everything will turn out okay but that God will hold you even when everything isn't.

The Lord often speaks to me through music, and during those days of extreme stress, with so much of our journey uncertain, an old tune floated through my mind. It is called the "Benediction" or "Doxology." The words originate from Numbers 6:23–26 when the Lord spoke to Moses. "Tell Aaron and his sons, 'This is how you are to bless the Israelites. You should say to them, "May the Lord bless you and protect you; May the Lord make his face shine on you and be gracious to you; May the Lord look with favor on you and give you peace."'"

I once heard a pastor say it's an "ear worm" when our thoughts bring melodies and words into our consciousness— melodies that we start humming in the car or around the house.

CHAPTER 8

Inpatient Therapy

It was the last week of January, and Tim's condition remained stable. He hadn't experienced any more emergency episodes. His trach was in place, along with his feeding tube, and we had grown accustomed to the constant rhythm of the ventilator and the beeping of the monitors. We had even become used to his unresponsiveness when the doctor checked him with a pinch or by drawing a finger up the bottom of his foot.

As our family kept vigil by his bedside, we were asked to watch for any changes such as a flicker of an eyelid or any kind of involuntary movement. Meanwhile, the MeritCare staff continued their search for a skilled rehabilitation facility in a three-state area.

One day while sitting by his bedside reading, I looked up to see that his beautiful, deep blue eyes were open. I began to speak to him, but his eyes were empty and unfocused. In an instant, his eyes closed, and he was gone. Under normal circumstances, we sometimes overlook the light and energy that come through someone's eyes. My son's open eyes that day were like pulling back the curtain to his inner self. In the coming days, he opened and closed his eyes occasionally and also began to make random arm movements, throwing back the sheet that covered him. I would cover him up and sometimes stroke his hand to calm him.

On January 26, a neuropsychologist came into the room and said Tim would be moved the following day to a facility that could accommodate all his needs. He would be transported by ambulance to a larger city four hours away. He mentioned that Tim would have two attendants traveling with him and asked if I would also ride in the ambulance. He stated that although Tim was still in an unresponsive state, he could hear me and that I might help keep him calm during the ambulance ride. I called my husband to share the news, and we alerted our other children and members of our vigil team that our location was changing.

The next day, January 27, I took my first ambulance ride. I followed Tim's gurney with all his gear down the elevator to the ambulance bay. His doctor walked with me and said, "Just talk to him like you always do and try to keep him from flailing around too much." He added, "The inside of the ambulance is pretty tight." We shook hands, and as the ambulance doors opened, he patted my shoulder and told me to get in and sit on the bench in the front. I did as he directed, and the gurney was pushed in up to my knees while the two attendants arranged things with one person seated on either side of the gurney.

As the doors closed from the outside and the ambulance pulled away from MeritCare, I thought, *I sure hope my son will listen to me if he gets restless because there isn't any room in here for throwing your arms around.*

We were only gone about half an hour when Tim began to move. The only place on his body where I could touch him was his forehead, so I placed my hand there and said, "Tim, it's Mom. You lie still now and be calm." To my surprise, it actually worked, and he was still for a few minutes. During the almost-four-hour drive, I must have spoken those words several hundred times as my son stilled and thrashed, stilled and thrashed over and over again.

When your loved one is unresponsive, it can feel like your presence is wasted, especially when they don't seem to register your voice or touch. But no matter how unresponsive they seem, know that you are an important part of your loved one's recovery. Your patience, voice, and touch are recognized as that unique and special gift only you can offer. The Bible teaches us that patience is an important aspect of our relationship with God and with others. Some well-known verses about patience are found in James 1:3–4: "Because you know that the testing of your faith produces endurance. And let endurance have its full effect, so that you may be mature and complete, lacking nothing." Stay strong, be patient, and pray.

I felt relieved when we arrived in the ambulance bay at the new facility because I needed to stretch, and Tim needed some space. The doors opened as new faces pulled the gurney out of the ambulance, and I followed it into a completely new institution, the skilled care rehabilitation facility that MeritCare had identified for us.

We rode up the elevator into a large room filled with sunshine that beamed through a bank of windows at the far end. The curtains were open, revealing the city skyline. The walls were a soft blue, and the bed in the center of the room was covered with a multicolored bedspread of gentle blue, mauve, and soft yellow. A metal frame across the head of the bed was used for lifting and moving an immobile patient. There was a chair and side table on either side of the bed, along with a bathroom at the far end. The attendants pulled the gurney up to the side of the bed, lifted Tim's limp body onto it, and then adjusted all his gear. The room was alive with light, sound, and gentle colors that softened the droning of the machines that accompanied Tim.

My husband had followed the ambulance. He entered the room shortly after we arrived. We were sitting beside Tim when a therapist and a doctor joined us. They greeted us and said, "If Tim can be awakened, we will do it; however, please don't be alarmed by how aggressive we are." We didn't understand what they meant and must have looked a little shocked as they explained further. "We will monitor him closely and begin a multidisciplinary approach to his care. Our first goal is to wean him from the ventilator. Our team of physicians, physical therapists, occupational therapists, speech-language pathologists, respiratory therapists, and dietitians will all play a role in his care."

We spent that first night in a nearby hotel. We were cautiously hopeful that Tim would wake up and come back to us. We discussed the large team of professionals with their varied skills who would be caring for our son. We questioned how they might approach weaning him off the ventilator and how the other disciplines would assist in his recovery. We had no answers, only questions, but we were impressed by the confidence of the doctors we had met.

The next morning, we walked into his room as the staff brought in a backboard that was slipped under his entire body. They rearranged the tubes still attached to him as they secured him head to toe on the board. Using a lifting machine, they stood him up beside the bed. The process of getting everything organized took much longer than the actual standing period, but we were told that this was the first step in trying to wake him up. They said he needed to be reminded that he was meant to be upright, not lying down.

During the first week of February, they successfully weaned Tim from the ventilator and had longer standing-up periods. Tim's eyes occasionally opened, but he didn't seem to focus. Once the ventilator was removed and all tubes except the feeding tube were taken out, they began sitting him up on the side of the bed. It was interesting that he kept tipping to one side and needed adjusting. He needed guidance on finding his center. We were informed that his brain could not determine the center at that point.

His room continued to be busy with light and soft music. We were encouraged to speak directly to him and to one another. The cards kept pouring in, and we read them to him before covering his walls with all the greetings and well wishes. We decorated his entire room with cards, pictures, and some of his favorite caps and other items from home.

The second week of February had a day to remember as our middle son and I sat on either side of Tim's bed. Tim's eyes were open as he turned to his brother and with very mushy speech said, "Where is my wallet?" Both of us were in shock as we first tried to determine what he was saying, and then we began to cry because we realized that he was thinking—actually thinking. That was the first day of the rest of Tim's life and ours as well. Until that day, we had been told he had brain activity, but we didn't know how much of his cognitive abilities had been impacted.

You have your own story of watching and waiting for that moment when hope returns. You may feel frustrated by how long it takes and fearful that what you hope for won't happen. You may be surprised or sad when your loved one does not come back as the person you knew before that fateful day. The first few weeks of our experience were filled with fear that our son would not survive and then fear that he would never be responsive again. Sometimes people feel frustration with these situations; other times there is anger toward people or God for this situation occurring at all. These are normal feelings, and it's okay to be sad, frustrated, or angry. Just know that God is still there, waiting to guide and support you.

Psalm 27:14 says, "Wait for the Lord; be strong, and let your heart be courageous." These words can uplift you with the hope that you can and will be strong with the Lord by your side.

The really hard work began the very next day. Tim spent three to four hours in therapy each day. He needed to learn how to find his center while sitting and then how to swallow so the feeding tube could be removed. His tongue had been severely injured in the accident, and now he needed to learn how to articulate his words properly.

He received therapy for speaking, counting, reading, sitting, standing, and walking. He underwent therapy focused on appropriate behavior in various situations and learned how to count money and manipulate objects. Later, he had lessons on reading recipes and cooking, writing, telling time, dressing himself, and managing personal care. We were informed that he had lost all the physical, emotional, and behavioral skills a child acquires through practice, instruction, or suggestion, and he needed to relearn them all.

Our family continued to join him as often as possible, and he was rarely without someone by his side. We were filled with joy and hope as the weeks passed, and he never wavered or complained about the hard work. His positive attitude continued to emerge more and more each day. He had always been a strong person with a sense of determination, and we were so thankful for that.

There was a large whiteboard with a big black marker hanging from it on the wall directly across from Tim's bed. As the therapy continued, we were told to record any of Tim's new skills or activities that we noticed. One day in early February, our daughter and son-in-law were spending some time with Tim. He had always worn a cap, so his sister handed one to him and asked him to put it on and take it off, which he did.

This was a new skill of listening, taking direction, and doing what was asked. Our daughter wrote these words on the whiteboard: "Tim can put his cap on and take it off." About a week later, my husband and I were with Tim when he began to focus on the whiteboard. He said in very mushy speech, "Tim can put his cap on and take it off." Then he paused, slowly turned his head to look at me, and said, "Big deal." We laughed until we cried as we became surer that he was really thinking.

As February progressed, Tim's personality continued to emerge. One day, he was feeling his head and face and asked for a mirror. I gave him a handheld mirror, which he held shakily up to his face. He touched the back of his head where a bald spot had formed from weeks of the cervical collar rubbing against it. He touched the still-healing scar on his throat where the trach had been and then opened his mouth to feel the line of cracked teeth. After a moment, he focused a bit more and said, "My eyes are crossed." I replied, "Yes they are, but the doctors tell us that can be corrected a little later, so don't worry about it." He smiled a cracked-tooth, cross-eyed smile, closed his eyes, and took a nap.

Another day in February, we arrived a little later in the day, knowing our middle son had been visiting. It was past the therapy timeline, but neither of them was in Tim's room or the family room. We asked the nurses where Tim was, and they said his brother had taken him for a ride in the wheelchair. We sat waiting in his room until finally they came rolling in with goofy smirks on both their faces. Tim said in his mushy speech, "I needed a smoke," grinning with his cracked teeth and still mischievous crossed eyes. We shook our heads.

In late February as therapy progressed to more challenging cognitive skills, I accompanied him to a session with his speech-language therapist. He was asking Tim how to spell and read a variety of words. Tim read a few and spelled a few, but as the session continued, Tim said, "I wasn't good at spelling before my accident; why do you think I could spell better now?" The therapist looked at me and then at Tim and said, "You know, you are right. Maybe we will try something else." They played a matching game with some success and more fun.

As the weeks progressed, we were able to take Tim out on short excursions. He was still unable to walk well, so we used a wheelchair. One afternoon we went to see a movie, and on the first day of March, we took Tim to the state wrestling tournament. Tim had wrestled throughout high school and college and was excited to witness the competition. The movie theater raised our awareness of the need for accessible door openers. The trip to the wrestling tournament provided an even greater realization of the difficulties faced by those with special needs.

We wheeled Tim into the stadium and took the elevator up to a viewing area. We noticed that people didn't automatically step aside for his chair. We observed that some individuals became upset when we asked them to sit so Tim could see over their heads. We found that the area designated for wheelchairs wasn't automatically recognized, and people stood in those spots. We all enjoyed the day together, but we have never forgotten our observations and lessons we learned that day. We became much more aware of the need to pay attention when people need assistance and to extend patience to those with physical or specific needs. We decided that the best way to promote that understanding is to set an example through our own behavior, patience, and helpfulness.

As March progressed, Tim became the greeter both in therapy and on the hospital floor. When we accompanied him to therapy, he would proudly introduce everyone and offer a wave or some kind of wisecrack. On the hospital floor, he could often be found in his chair or practicing his walking skills, peeking into various rooms to visit and offer encouragement to other patients. His positive attitude was contagious, and as always, he made friends wherever he went.

On March 9, Tim's church and community held a fundraiser for him with hundreds of people in attendance. We were able to bring Tim out of the hospital for the weekend so he could attend the event. He was still in a wheelchair facing many challenges, but his outgoing personality shone as he quivered to get out of the chair to stand and greet those who had come to support him. He smiled with his cracked teeth and crossed eyes, shaking hands until he was exhausted.

Toward the end of March, Tim had plateaued, having reached the limits of what inpatient therapy could achieve, and they were going to discharge him. The weeks had flown by quickly, and he had progressed from being unresponsive to eating without assistance and completing some simple tasks. As discharge plans began, the social worker met with us to provide a list of long-term care facilities in the area. She mentioned that those facilities would continue his therapy and we could visit him. We did not consider this option. Instead, we quickly updated our home to accommodate his needs. We added extra handrails, reconfigured the walk-in shower, and made room for the wheelchair as we moved into the next phase of traumatic brain injury recovery.

God in the Midst of TBI – When God Awakens You

We were just starting to awaken to the realization that the remarkable progress we had witnessed was merely the beginning of a true recovery. We were beginning to comprehend that three months was only a brief moment on this incredible journey. And we were starting to see that God had brought us this far, but there was so much more ahead. The questions below were running through my mind while Tim was making his recovery and how we sought to answer those same questions during the process.

- *How amazing is God's creation of a human brain that can heal itself over time?* We were in awe of all the healing accomplished by Tim, his doctors, and most importantly, God.
- *How do we maintain a work-life balance?* We reflected on how our whole family, our colleagues, and our communities had come together to support us this far, yet we still wanted to sit down and take a nap.
- *How can we support our entire family while devoting so much energy to this child?* We recognized that all our children were supportive of the attention Tim needed at this time. Still, we worried about the strain on everyone, especially our youngest son.
- *How do we guide our son while stepping back to allow him to find himself?* We were just starting to realize that the responsibility for continual improvement rested entirely on Tim, and all we could do was observe and offer support.

You might be at a similar point in your journey with a traumatic situation. You may feel incredibly grateful that your loved one has come this far and that you have also survived. However, you understand that there is still so much more to do, and the outcome remains uncertain.

Walking through TBI, there's much that makes us look back and wonder how far the Lord has brought us, even though there is still so far to go. I am reminded of David's prayer in 1 Chronicles 17:16 where it reads, "Then King David went in, sat in the Lord's presence, and said, 'Who am I, Lord God, and what is my house that you have brought me this far?'"

Although there is much in his life that David could lament, he humbles himself before God in recognition of the grace and blessings he has received. When we consider our own struggles and those faced by our loved ones during recovery, we can choose to be consumed by the tragedy around us and in our lament ask God, "Why did you do this to me?" Or we can be consumed by the mercy God has poured out on us and ask, "Who am I, Lord God, and what is my house that you have brought me this far?" (1 Chron. 17:16).

Leaning on God for strength and courage each and every day is how I navigate life. It feels normal and natural to me. I was born into a family of believers and am blessed to have a deep and abiding faith that God loves me and has my back no matter what happens. You may or may not share that same depth of faith. If you are a person of faith, I encourage you to lean into it. Talk to God about your struggles, and let Him carry you when needed. If you haven't had God in your life or haven't talked to Him for a while, know that He is still there waiting for you to reach out. The beauty of our God is that He loves you unconditionally and is just waiting for you to love Him back.

Consider these questions as you move forward on your own journey:

1. How do you recognize thankfulness amid all this trauma?
2. How do you dig deeply to keep hope alive when the final outcome remains uncertain?
3. Where can you find the well of patience and understanding to draw from?

CHAPTER 9
Outpatient Therapy

My husband and I arrived at the rehabilitation hospital on Wednesday, March 12, to begin the next step on our journey. We brought two large boxes of chocolates with us that day. The first box we left at the desk on the floor where Tim had been. We said our goodbyes and expressed our gratitude for everything they had done. As we left the hospital floor, Tim reminded us that he wanted to go down to the therapy area one last time so he could bring the candy and say goodbye to everyone there. We were happy to accompany him and say our own goodbyes. We enjoyed watching him give hugs and words of thanks to everyone.

We met a staff member at the exit door, loaded Tim into our vehicle, and headed home with a list of tasks to complete in the upcoming weeks. We already had appointments for outpatient therapy scheduled. We needed to make a new appointment with an eye doctor to help correct his crossed eyes, see a dentist for his broken teeth, and visit a psychologist to discuss his mental health. As Tim recovered, appointments, doctor visits, and waiting rooms would be part of our lives for the foreseeable future.

During the two-hour drive, we updated Tim on what to expect next and the upcoming appointments. We discussed which bedroom he would be in and the activities his little brother was involved in. He had regained some of his witty personality and shared stories about people who had visited him, phone calls he had received, and his favorite therapists. When we stopped at the local pharmacy, he wanted to come in to pick up his prescriptions. He was determined to walk despite his unsteady gait, and he totally disregarded any second glances from other customers.

As our garage door opened and we drove inside, I felt a wave of relief knowing we had come this far and that Tim was home with us. He had accomplished so much, even though there was still more work and healing ahead. I pondered the miracle we had witnessed and was humbled by the gracious gift the Lord had given us.

Psalm 77:14 reads, "You are the God who works wonders; you revealed your strength among the peoples." I believe miracles happen every day if we are watching for them. The healing of our son was a significant miracle as we witnessed God's hand on him to heal his body and his brain. You have your own miracles. I encourage you to notice them and give thanks for them. I believe that by acknowledging the miracles at work in our lives, we can find hope and strength through trusting in God's faithful presence in every circumstance. When we know He's there, we can turn to Him to sustain us. Even now, He can sustain you.

The human body and brain offer a spectacular view into God's creation of all things. The brain can rebuild its connections, strengthen weakened parts caused by injury, and heal itself as God designed it to. As I observe this miracle, I am reminded of the words of King David in Psalm 139:13-14: "For it was you who created my inward parts; you knit me together in my mother's womb. I will praise you because I have been remarkably and wondrously made." I know that every journey has different outcomes, but I urge you to consider that wherever you and your loved ones are on your journey, you are God's creation. He has made you remarkable and wondrous, and only He knows the plans He has for you.

We opened the front door of our home and helped Tim up the stairs to the main floor. To accommodate Tim, we had made some updates and renovations to the house. My husband had installed handrails on both sides of the stairways in our home, and we had rearranged some of our furniture for easier movement. We completed some updates to our lower level so our younger son, a seventh grader, had his own space and bathroom. My husband also updated the master shower so it would work well for Tim.

Tim walked around our home, seemingly enjoying the simple pleasure of just being there. We confirmed which room would be his, and he went in and lay down on the bed. As I peeked in and quietly closed the door, I saw that he was asleep.

My husband's business needed his attention, and we were accustomed to his being away several days during the week, so we all agreed that he should return to a more normal routine. I was able to keep my flexible work schedule and was happy to handle things at home.

The days began to tick by as we settled into this new routine. During the first few weeks, my day started at 4:00 a.m. with prayer and journaling. Then I woke up my youngest son for breakfast and got him to the bus for school. I prepared myself for the day, woke Tim, went to work by 7:30 a.m., left work at 9:45 a.m., picked up Tim, and took him to therapy. After returning to work, I picked up Tim from therapy around 1:00 p.m., settled him at home, went back to work until 4:30 p.m., and then came home to make dinner, check on our seventh grader's homework, attend any evening activities, do laundry, review shopping needs or upcoming appointments, make sure Tim was settled and his alarm was on. And then I fell into bed.

The therapists encouraged us to attend a local support group for brain injury, and Tim agreed to go. One evening, we walked into the meeting room where a large table was in the center, surrounded by about twenty folding chairs. There was a variety of people with different degrees of obvious injury and capabilities. They welcomed us as someone spoke up and directed the group to go around the table and introduce themselves. Most of the people appeared familiar with each other, and they all shared a little of their own stories.

Tim shared that he had recently been in the hospital and was now doing outpatient therapy. Someone asked how long it had been since the accident. We said it had been about three months, and the entire group said, "Oh, you are just a baby." I remember feeling a little defensive when they made that comment, thinking back to all the struggles and healing we had already gone through. I also remember pondering the idea of being at the beginning of this journey rather than the end. At that moment, however, I could only focus on the present, so I brushed the thought aside.

The group continued by sharing local activities and fundraisers or additional support activities that were available. I found it interesting to talk with other caregivers and learn about services that could help. We attended the next meeting and appreciated meeting others who had similar experiences. However, as we drove home that second time, Tim said, "Mom, I don't want to go back there." I asked why, and he said he was ready to move on and not dwell on what happened. He didn't want to look back but rather look forward.

I was not surprised by Tim's thoughts and words because that was his usual approach to life. I agreed, and we stopped attending the support group. Still, I was very thankful for our brief time with them because I took away one important realization from that encounter: Three months are nothing in the timeline of TBI recovery. In fact, one person in that group suggested that ten years would be a good milestone to aim for. Looking back now, that marker was certainly true.

As I became more comfortable leaving Tim at home, I searched for other ways to get him to and from therapy. I found out about a bus system that offered door-to-door service with pick-up and drop-off help. I paid for their services, and even though I was fearful about Tim traveling independently, he had no reservation about doing it.

As Tim seemed to be managing his schedule, I backed off to give him more autonomy while still staying very watchful. We changed his therapy schedule to a slightly later time in the day so I could occasionally observe him or pick him up afterward.

On one particular day, we agreed that I would pick him up and he should not ride the bus home; however, things didn't go as planned, and Tim went missing and as the minutes passed, I lost my normally calm and commanding demeanor. I turned into what I call *crazy mom* as I temporarily lost my perspective and panicked.

I left work, drove to the therapy building, pulled up to the sidewalk bench to pick him up, and saw that he was not there. I parked my car and went inside to ask the desk attendant if Tim had been there that day. The attendant said yes but that his session was over and he had left. I tried to stay calm as the hair on the back of my neck stood up. I went back to the car and drove home, glancing side to side, searching for a sign of my son. At home, I called the bus service and asked if they had picked him up. They said they had brought him to therapy but that he was not waiting when the bus stopped after therapy. I went into a full-blown frenzy, got back in my car, and drove the three and a half miles from our house to the therapy facility, using every route I could think of.

I came back home and called my husband who was working nearby. He headed home immediately. I sat at home for a few minutes and then called the police department and said in my crazy mom screech, "My son has a brain injury and I can't find him. If he is walking, he looks wobbly like he is drunk, but he is not; he has a brain injury." The dispatcher kindly and calmly said she would alert the local patrols to watch for him.

I couldn't sit at home, so I got back in my car and drove in another direction, looking out the window for him. I was frantic. With no sign of him anywhere, I went back home, and as I drove into our driveway, I saw someone sitting in the swing on our front porch. I parked the car, walked around the corner, and saw Tim sitting in the swing smoking a cigarette.

Crazy mom felt relieved, angry, and embarrassed all at the same time. I stared at him as he said, "I decided to walk home because I wanted a smoke, and I knew you wouldn't get me any. I stopped at the gas station." I asked him how he knew the way home from the therapy location as it was an unfamiliar area with some streets having no sidewalks. He said, "Mom, I am paying attention." His eyes twinkled, and he flashed that quizzical smile of his. Shortly after, my husband and the police patrol car drove in, and I had to admit to a false alarm and crazy mom syndrome.

One day we stopped to fill a prescription at our local pharmacy. Tim usually wanted to come inside with me because he enjoyed talking to the pharmacist and doing a little shopping. That day, he said he wanted to stay in the car. I was nervous that he might walk away, so I locked the car doors and took the keys as I stepped out and went into the store.

When I returned to the car about twenty minutes later, Tim asked, "Mom, why did you lock me in the car?" I looked at him as he continued, "I know where I am, I'm not going to walk away, you know." I was just starting to realize that I needed to let go and let him be a grown man. I needed to accept that in time he would live his own life, make his own mistakes, and step back into the world in his own way.

When we face life's trials, it can take time to regain a sense of trust and joy. We might harbor feelings of dread and believe we can't overcome the obstacles in front of us. We may worry that God isn't paying attention to our needs. Sometimes we have an occasional panic attack and feel like a crazy mom has replaced us.

I believe these are completely normal human behaviors and feelings. I realize that by trying to control Tim's activities and safety, I was short-circuiting my ability to trust and appreciate the capabilities he was demonstrating. I also know that turning to God can help us regain that sense of peace and control. Raising your voice to God and telling Him that your burden is too heavy actually helps lift the load.

In Matthew 11:28–30, Jesus tells us to bring our burdens to him through these words, "Come to me, all of you who are weary and burdened, and I will give you rest. Take my yoke upon you and learn from me, because I am lowly and humble in heart, and you will find rest for your souls. For my yoke is easy and my burden is light."

I encourage you to take Jesus at His word and give Him the burden you can't carry. The truth is, there's much we can't control as caregivers to someone with TBI, and the control freak inside of us often reminds us of the limits of our own influence. We can't make our loved ones better. We can't predict how they'll respond. We can't rush the recovery process.

Sometimes we feel overwhelmed by the things we can't control and are tempted to try to control things even more. Yet all that does is give us more gray hairs and a deeper awareness of our weaknesses. Jesus invites us to release what we were never meant to carry and let Him bear our burdens instead.

As Tim continued his therapy and his home routines became more stable, another facet of traumatic brain injury recovery started to appear. Tim became increasingly impatient and critical of his little brother. He made cryptic remarks, criticized his brother's behavior and experiences, and was generally unkind to the same little brother he used to be so proud of. We were told that traumatic brain injury can lead to personality and behavioral changes. Those changes can range from difficulties with social situations and managing emotions to impacts on cognitive functions, all of which can put strain on relationships.

My husband and I intervened and talked with Tim about his words and actions toward his little brother and other family members. Over time, Tim became more thoughtful about what he said and did in various situations.

Research on the impact of TBI on non-injured siblings shows both negative and positive effects. Negative effects may include difficulty adjusting to new family dynamics, anger and stress caused by the changes, anxiety, emotional withdrawal, and feelings of being left out, isolated, or neglected. On the other hand, positive effects can include increased empathy and caring, improved social skills and communication, stronger family bonds and a sense of unity, a deeper understanding of life and resilience, and a heightened awareness of others. As Tim and our youngest son worked on their relationship, we observed positive changes not only in our youngest son but also in ourselves as we grew as a family and learned to care for each other in greater ways.

As a family, we all related to these various emotions and adjustments from time to time. Over the years, my husband and I encouraged our children to talk with each other about what happened during those early months and subsequent years.

Occasionally, we find ourselves as a family reminiscing about that period, and our home is filled with funny stories and laughter.

While we can laugh about that time now, we understand that not every family will experience the healing ours has. If members of your family are struggling to cope with life in a post-TBI world, invite them to share their struggles with you when they feel ready. Although we know the effects of someone's TBI go far beyond the individual, it is wise as caregivers to be attentive to those who are experiencing the ripple effects of life after a traumatic brain injury.

Tim made progress in therapy. He focused on walking with a steadier gait. He worked with a speech therapist as his severely injured tongue from the accident continued to heal, improving his speech articulation. He also worked on building strength for his left-sided weakness and enhancing his fine and gross motor skills. Additionally, he practiced decision-making, judgment, and appropriate behavior in a variety of situations.

The therapists offered suggestions on what they called coping skills—tools to incorporate into daily life that would help Tim manage things such as schedules, appointments, bills, and groceries. Tim did not hesitate to try these new tools and was eager to suggest that we use them as well. The suggestions might seem like common sense or routine for many of us, but they were new to Tim.

Tim returned from therapy almost every day with new ideas on how to improve his ability to handle daily life. His memory was not what it used to be, so he needed to use external strategies. We bought sticky notes, magnets for the fridge, pens, and pads of paper. He made lists of what he had to do each day, what time he wanted to get up, what chores he needed to do, where he had placed certain items, who he wanted to call, and more. His life became very organized and structured, and whenever it unraveled, he felt frustrated and upset.

He had trouble waking up in the morning and learned about an alarm clock that could be placed under the mattress. It would both ring and vibrate. We found out where they were sold, and he loved the idea of waking up his brain in the morning. That alarm was so loud and vibrated so much that the entire house would wake up. We laughed about it when we all wanted to be awake, but if it rang when we were trying to sleep, there was no laughter.

As we followed up on all the appointments, Tim got some glasses with prisms that helped correct his crossed eyes. He had multiple dental visits to restore his great smile. One appointment that was especially memorable was the meeting with a psychologist. We drove two hours to this appointment and talked about what was going to happen next, such as testing for a driver's license, getting ready for the construction season to start, and more.

We sat down in front of the doctor's big desk, and the kind man asked Tim a variety of questions about how he was doing, what he was up to, how he was feeling, if he was taking his medication, and what his plans were. The final question was this: "Are you depressed?" I watched Tim's face as he furrowed his brow and said, "No. Why would I be depressed?" That was the last time we saw that particular doctor since Tim's personality would not accept anything less than moving forward and getting back to life.

God in the Midst of TBI – When God Journeys with You

Toward the end of April, the outpatient therapist called to ask me to stop by. I arrived feeling pleased with Tim's progress and eager to see what they would work on next. When I arrived, I saw Tim working with someone at the far end of the therapy area. A receptionist ushered me into an office, asked me to sit, and said someone would be there shortly. I was confused because in the past, I had just joined Tim and watched him complete the various requirements.

The director of the program entered the office and sat down. He looked at me with a melancholy expression and said, "We feel that Tim has plateaued in his recovery at this point, and we will be exiting him from our program at the end of the week." As tears filled my eyes and my voice began to shake, I asked with sorrow and shock, "But Tim is not well yet. He is not himself. He is not ready to live independently."

I asked what we were supposed to do next. The director's answer was completely shocking to me because the words he had been spoken throughout the last few months had not truly registered in my mind until that moment. He said, "There is nothing more to do except wait and watch." He added, "You will continue to see changes in personality and capabilities in every way over the coming years." He said that the final outcome was still unknown, and no other therapy would be of value.

So now what?

The news that medical professionals can do nothing more to heal your loved one is shocking. Our instinct is to believe that once the doctors and therapists finish their work, everything will return to normal. The reality is that the rest of the work depends on the individual and on God. Once again, we needed prayer, patience, trust, and limitless love.

A message by well-known evangelist Billy Graham in his journaling devotional book *Hope for Each Day* offers acknowledgment of the trial you're going through and courage that you'll come out better on the other side.

> There are two ways of getting out of a trial. One is to simply try to get rid of the trial, and be thankful when it is over. The other is to recognize the trial as a challenge from God to claim a larger blessing than we have ever had. Sometimes God removes our trials, and it isn't necessarily wrong to ask Him to do that. But often the trails remain, and when they do, we should accept them and ask God to teach us from them.

As Peter Marshall, another well-known evangelist once put it, "God will not permit any troubles to come upon us, unless He has a specific plan by which great blessing can come out of the difficulty."

We have moved from the shock of sudden injury through the fearful acute care, past the grueling first relearning processes, and on to the end of professional expertise and support. It is remarkable that now more than ever we turn to God for continued healing, courage, and sustained stamina for our son and for wisdom for ourselves. Looking back, we can see God throughout our entire journey with TBI. We see Him in the ambulance caring for Tim through the paramedic. We see Him in the ER where doctors did whatever was necessary. We see Him in his hospital room as family and friends showered Tim with gifts and affection. We see Him in the therapy and doctor appointments as He healed Tim's body and mind.

It's a long journey, and no matter where you are in it, I encourage you to trust in God. He has a plan for you and your loved one. Please remember that "great blessing can come out of the difficulty." As you endure the journey before you, trust that God is journeying with you.

CHAPTER 10
Life After TBI

The outpatient therapy was over, and Tim was discharged. For the family, there is a curious sense of confusion and panic when healthcare professionals say they are finished with their work. Until that point, we clung to the idea that they were fixing our loved one. Somehow, we don't or can't hear the words that therapy is just the start of the TBI recovery journey and that the even greater issue of recovery is unpredictable and not sequential. The world continues to move on, professionals look forward to helping the next patient, and friends and family assume that everything is fine. My husband and I struggled with this next step as we and our son set out on our own to navigate what was coming next.

It was mid-June, and we could look back far enough to realize that we had experienced a healing miracle. From the night of the accident through near-death experiences to fighting back into responsiveness and relearning every aspect of living, we had watched the hand of God move upon our son. Yet he was not fully restored, and we did not think he was ready to live independently or reenter his former work life. We also knew he was remembering the person he had been and not yet able to accept the new person who was emerging.

When our loved ones are struggling to survive catastrophic change, it's hard to know what to do. We have more questions and concerns than answers. Healthcare professionals are no longer a resource telling us what will happen next or how we should react. For us, the nagging questions are at the forefront of our minds. What will happen to our son? What is next for him? What will he do for work? What are we supposed to do to be helpful? Perhaps you are having the same thoughts and concerns. The answer is neither simple nor what you might have hoped for. The answer is that time will tell.

Over the months, our family had become familiar with brain injuries that ranged from less severe to much more severe than our son's. We met families whose loved ones were able to return home in just a few weeks and others who mourned because their loved ones would never get to go home again. We felt grateful yet perplexed as we turned to God and prayed for the strength and wisdom to let go. This new reality was the hardest time of all, and it might be for you as well. We cling to the words from Isaiah 41:10: "Do not fear, for I am with you; do not be afraid for I am your God."

We soon realized that although our minds were filled with questions and concerns about Tim's ability to navigate life independently, Tim's mind was focused on the next steps—with determination and relentless grit. He had a plan and was determined to move forward. He remembered his career and the skills he had developed, and was committed to returning to the work he enjoyed so much.

He had spent ten years in the heavy construction industry. He was skilled at operating large machinery as if they were an extension of his own arm. He possessed the eye-hand coordination to manipulate the delicate toggles of heavy equipment to move dirt and lay infrastructure pipe for water and sewer with precision. He had earned the trust of those working in trenches more than 6 feet deep and had the knowledge to get the job done efficiently and skillfully. He was sought after in this industry for his skills and was laser-focused on getting back to that work.

While he was in the hospital, his boss called to wish him well and said he was welcome back whenever he was ready. In Tim's mind, he was ready. We suggested that he wait, take a year off work, and rest his mind, giving himself time to think about his next steps, but he wouldn't hear of it. He stayed in our home, followed a daily routine, and made plans for what was next. We gave him suggestions when he asked for them, but we did little to help him. Over the next six weeks, we watched as he put his plans into motion.

The first hurdle was getting his driver's license back. One day when I returned from work, he announced that he had called and scheduled a driving test. I thought it was too soon, but I took him to the test, which he failed. Over the next month, he took the test three more times and finally succeeded. That meant he needed his truck, and he was driving again. He called his boss and decided that he would return to full-time work by early August. The date was set, and he was determined to meet it no matter what we said.

Time passed quickly from mid-June to early August as he prepared to get his life back. He had visits from coworkers and friends. He watched television with his phone nearby just as he always did, knowing someone might call or visit at any moment. However, for the first time in his life, the phone did not ring as often. He had been out of circulation, life was busy, and changes in Tim were clear. Sometimes his friends didn't know what to say.

During his inpatient recovery, the therapists and doctors warned him that he must avoid any activities where he might sustain another blow to the head. He took this warning seriously and made arrangements to sell his motorcycle and snowmobile. He would never ride them again. Instead, he purchased an ice fishing house, and in the following years during the winter months when he was off from work, he spent many happy days fishing with Grandpa and others.

When the return-to-work date arrived, Tim did not hesitate. He packed his bag, his vibrating alarm clock, and pushed into the heavily populated metropolitan area. The initial welcome back to work was great, and we were so happy for him; however, it did not go well, and soon he was back at our house looking for another job. His industry connections opened many doors, so he was able to find new work very quickly, and he pushed forward.

Over the next eleven years, he started new work that ended and started again and again. He found different ways to cope as he began to peel back his new reality. He looked for jobs in his field that were less demanding on his fine motor skills. He hired a friend to pay his bills and handle maintenance on his rural home. Whenever possible, he brought his camper closer to the work sites and stayed in his uncle's backyard. He mapped out each job site the night before so he would feel more comfortable with the roads, traffic patterns, detours, and other variables.

Sometimes it seemed like a particular job was the right fit, and he would work a season or two. But then something would go wrong, and it would end. Each time he returned to us, our hearts broke for him, but still he kept trying. His personality and disposition were still healing and developing, which made the struggle even more challenging as he questioned decisions and processes in certain situations of his assigned work. He remembered his own expertise and told us he knew exactly how to do the work, but his eye-hand coordination would not cooperate. He was frustrated, angry, and eventually for the first time, sad.

Once he called from another state and said he was coming home. We waited fitfully for his return, and when he walked in the door, his eyes filled with tears for the first time since his accident. He said, "I was let go. I just can't do it. I guess I'm just going to have to be disabled." Our hearts ached for our son as his limitless determination and spirit seemed to be breaking.

We watched as he continued to interact with old friends and made new ones, just as he always had. However, there were two people who encouraged him the most. The first one was his brother who was four years younger than Tim. He knew Tim so well that he could pull him out of sadness and persuade him to keep going. The other one was an amazing, loyal, lifelong friend who never wavered and was always there for Tim. That friend visited often, called, took Tim on road trips, made arrangements for fishing and hunting adventures, encouraged him to keep trying, and built up his self-confidence while ignoring his sometimes angry and argumentative outbursts.

We moved forward through the years, which included weddings, funerals, relationships, baptisms, and family gatherings. During that time, we watched Tim's outbursts and impulsive behaviors begin to shift. I remembered a comment from a therapist who said, "All the etiquette and social norms learned while growing up need to be relearned and refreshed." One teachable moment occurred at a wedding when Tim's impulse was to take off his shirt because he was too hot. That impulse was redirected as he realized that when you're too hot, you must keep your shirt on despite the heat and consider other options such as wearing sleeveless shirts.

After about a year, Tim had moved back to his own home full-time and regained his personal autonomy, and we were happy for him. The years went by, and from time to time, we looked back and commented on changes in his personality, his tolerance, and his coping skills. He was working, finding his way, and reestablishing his life. He had built a support system, structure, and organization that eased some of his stress. We offered support and suggestions when he asked for them. He lived in a familiar community that he loved, but we still felt uneasy about his future and the work he continued to strive for.

I remembered the words of the neuropsychologist in the ICU: "The recovery of TBI is complex because he will remember himself as he was before the accident, and as he gets to know and accept the new person, true healing will be accomplished." I also remember the comment from the people in the TBI support group we attended just four months after the accident. They had said in unison, "You are just a baby." And then there was the remark when he was discharged from outpatient therapy: "There is nothing more we can do. Now you must watch and wait, and over the coming years, you will see improvements—cognitive, emotional, and physical. However, he must do this work on his own."

Then one day, eleven years after the accident, God sent an angel in the form of a friend to share a work opportunity that Tim would never have considered until that very moment. There was a job opening in Tim's local community. It still involved dirt work but on local roads for local people with much less stress and more time to think things over. He went to the interview, was hired, and that day marked the first day of the rest of his life.

Since that day, Tim has changed jobs one more time, but he continues to work locally near his home with people who have known him for many years. He is trusted and respected for his good work and his work ethic. Life is good.

God in the Midst of TBI – When God Invites You to Walk by Faith

As I ponder the opportunity presented to Tim, I am certain that God's hand never left him. God had been watching and waiting for the moment when Tim was ready to see the new person who had risen from the ashes. There was always a plan and a time for that plan to unfold. What a marvelous mystery!

I believe that God's plan for our lives is a mysterious and unfolding narrative. God has a purpose for each of us, and the details are often unclear. That mystery is both a source of comfort and a challenge as believers because we strive to walk by faith, trusting that God's love and guidance will lead us.

"For we walk by faith, not by sight" (2 Cor. 5:7). The difficult part comes when that faith is tested. We walk by faith—a faith that can falter because we lose someone we love, struggle with our finances, or face terrible accidents. It can be hard to walk by faith.

"Not by sight" holds the deeper message. We often feel like we need to see what's coming next, plan ahead, and ensure there are no unexpected bumps in the road. We also want to be in control of our destiny. The fact is that we can't see our future, and we will definitely face unexpected challenges. We benefit when we return to that childlike, innocent faith. When we give God the reins to our lives, we can relax and follow His direction—when we walk by faith, not by sight.

When the road is hard and the burden is heavy, reach out and grasp the Lord's loving hand. When you are down on your knees and cannot take another step, let Him carry you. When you are drained of all your energy, joy, and hope, cry out to Him and ask Him to restore you. When you can't see which path to follow, pray "Father, increase my faith and help me trust You even though I cannot see where I'm going or what's coming next."

Every TBI situation is unique, and the recovery process can differ significantly. You might have a loved one who will not take no for an answer. You may have a loved one who submits to their new situation more easily. You may know someone who can't seem to overcome their circumstances or sees every obstacle as a burden rather than a challenge. The ebb and flow of a TBI victim's journey can also vary as they experience different successes and setbacks. There is no right or wrong way to live after such a traumatic event. There is only your way.

As I watched my son face his challenges, I believed that the best thing a caregiver can do is encourage, observe, listen, and then step back. I believe the survivor of a TBI benefits greatly from developing their own coping skills. They want and need to feel pride in themselves and their successes, and they must step into their new reality on their own and in their own way.

It has been twenty-three years since that fateful phone call, and we appreciate our son every single day. He is happy and healthy. He enjoys a rewarding work life, a rich social life, and is involved in many activities. He is quick to ask us how we are doing and invites us over to his home to grill a steak. He loves attending family events and is known for his great hugs.

As a family, we know we are truly blessed and have gained much from this powerful journey. We are all wiser and stronger because of it. We have witnessed miracles that strengthened our faith and increased our belief in the power of prayer. Most of all, we have learned to trust in God's healing and timing.

Ours is a success story. Tim is truly successful. He loves the Lord and has guided many people to learn about Jesus. He isn't afraid to encourage others to dig deep and overcome their hardships. He is strong-willed, opinionated, argumentative, loving, and kind—and we are so blessed to be his parents.

I once asked him if he saw the light, the heavenly light, during the weeks he was unresponsive. He said, "No, Mom, I didn't." I was a little disappointed because I had hoped he could tell me about it; however, as I reflect on the subsequent years, I realize that although he doesn't remember seeing the light, it shines through him. God has blessed him.

When we are in the midst of a crisis, it is natural to focus on the difficult and sad things. However, Ephesians 3:13 gives us a message from the Apostle Paul while he was a prisoner in Rome: "So, then I ask you not to be discouraged over my afflictions on your behalf, for they are your glory." This verse offers us humility and hope. We all face hardships in life, but Paul encourages us not to be discouraged but to persevere with faith, facing our challenges for God's glory and His greater plan.

If we keep this message in mind, it can help us view our situation as a challenge that glorifies God instead of a burden, a punishment, or abandonment by God. Thinking of our struggle this way shifts the perspective from being a victim of circumstances to being a victor over them.

Even in our crisis, Jesus promises to be with us and sustain us. "Come to me, all of you who are weary and burdened, and I will give you rest. Take my yoke upon you and learn from me, because I am lowly and humble in heart, and you will find rest for your souls" (Matt. 11:28–29). Jesus offers rest to those who trust Him, both physically and spiritually. He asks us to turn to Him and accept His guidance, comfort, and peace. He invites us to lean on Him. I love these verses because Jesus invites us to come to Him when we are weary. He says to take His yoke and learn from Him, which means choosing to walk with Him unburdened and humble, for it will give our souls rest.

Watching someone endure pain and suffering is tremendously difficult and makes us weary. When our loved ones struggle, we struggle too. When our children are hurting, we feel it as well. When our parents are sick, we feel sick inside. And when we lose someone dear, a part of us goes with them. We spend our energy trying to help, comfort, and support others, and that's a good thing. However, when that burden becomes too heavy, Jesus tells us exactly what to do. He says, "Come to me, . . . and I will give you rest."

I encourage you to set aside dedicated time each day to talk with Jesus and walk with Him. Whether you have a conversation or write your thoughts in a journal as I do, that habit becomes a stress release for your body, a cleansing for your mind, and a source of strength for your spirit. Go to Jesus when you are weary, and He will give you strength. Lean on Him, and He will teach you, guide you, and truly give you rest.

May God bless and keep you always.

www.ingramcontent.com/pod-product-compliance
Lightning Source LLC
Chambersburg PA
CBHW071810090426
42737CB00012B/2019